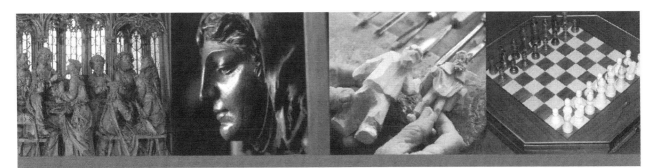

WOODCARVING
THE COMPLETE GUIDE

JOHANNES POULARD

The Complete Guide to Woodcarving

Johannes Poulard

Contents

Chapter One: The Basics of Woodcarving: Learn what the basics are. Types of woodcarving, including chip carving, relief carving, two dimensional carving, three dimensional carving. Learn the tools needed for woodcarving. Know the best woods for woodcarving and learn the difference between soft and hard woods.

Chapter Two: Chip Carving: One of the oldest and simplest types of woodcarving. Chip carving is carving chips out of the wood, making triangular, circular, semi circular, or oval notches in the wood to make a design. See photos and drawings of different folk designs done with chip carving.

Chapter Three: Relief Carving: Learn how to do relief carving. This is one of the more difficult types of woodcarving. Unlike chip carving, which is geometric, relief carving is more textured. Relief carving is the first step in doing two dimensional carving.

Chapter Four: Two Dimensional Carving: Learn what two dimensional carving is. Turn your relief carving into images, icons, and other amazing works of art.

Chapter Five: Three Dimensional Carving: Learn how to carve bowls and utensils, figurines out of blocks of wood. Learn how to carve birds, people, statues, etc. See the step-by-step process of carving wooden duck decoys, and more.

Chapter Six: Use of Woodcarving to Create your own Furniture: Learn how you can make tables, doors, cabinets, and other trinkets and furniture using both chip and relief carving. Learn how to work a lave to make those fancy bed posts or posts for a fence or railing.

Chapter Seven: Stains, Varnishes, and other Finishes: Learn how to properly varnish and stain your finished carved pieces. Learn how you can manipulate the color of your wood. Also, learn which stains can bring out the wood grain. Learn the difference between polyurethane varnishes and wood resins. Learn about proper sanding of surfaces.

Chapter Eight: Enhance your Woodcarving Using a Dremel Tool and other Power Tools: One of the most versatile and compact power tools which is popular among professional woodcarvers. Learn about using a jigsaw for more intricate carving pieces.

Chapter Nine: Chainsaw Carving: Have you ever thought of carving an entire tree trunk with a chainsaw. Were you ever amazed at carved totem poles and other yard decorations? This is the chapter for you.

Epilogue: Basic Review: Added extra tidbits to make your woodcarving experience more fun.

Chapter One

The basics of Woodcarving

One of the greatest forms of artwork is woodcarving. Woodcarving has been used over the millennia to create religious artifacts, folk designs, images, and more. Some woodcarving is two-dimensional and others is three dimensional. There are different levels of woodcarving which all require a certain level of skill to accomplish. These levels will all be covered in the upcoming chapters. What you will learn in this chapter are as follows:

A. **The different types of woodcarving:** You will understand the different types used in folk art and classical works as well. These types include chip carving, relief carving, two dimensional and three dimensional carving.
B. **Tools needed for basic woodcarving:** You will learn about the special knives needed for basic woodcarving. You will also understand a little bit about whittling with a pocket knife also. You will learn the difference between a chisel and a carving knife. Know when a piece of wood to be carved will be in need of a mallet and chisel and when a simple set of woodcarving knives are needed.
C. **The different types of woods** which are ideal for woodcarving. You will learn why basswood is the best wood to start with. You will also learn about other different woods, ranging from maple, cherry, walnut, oak, aspen, and pine.

The Different Types of Woodcarving
Being exposed to woodcarving, you will have access to the different types of woodcarving. Depending on your skill, you can pick and choose what type of woodcarving you would feel more comfortable working with. You can then move on to more complicated types of woodcarving.

Chip carving is basically the simplest technique of woodcarving and is often used in traditional folk art pieces throughout eastern Europe and Asia. Russians, Ukrainians, and Georgians are very well known for their chip carving styles, which can be developed into very ornate and intricate patterns. Chip carving is generally geometric in style, as most of the chips carved out are either triangular, square, or linear. Some circular lines can also be carved in a chip carved piece. See figure One below as an example of a work done in chip carving.

Figure One: Georgian traditional chip carving used on the doors for the stereo and fridge cabinet of this minibar.

Relief carving is what most people tend to think about when they think about woodcarving. Relief carving is the most common form of woodcarving practiced today. It does require a bit more skill than chip carving, as you are carving out more than mere chips from the wood. When done properly, the whole object of relief carving is to create the illusion of a three-dimensional image on a two-dimensional surface.

Unlike chip carving, where you simply carve out chips and simply leave a mark in an area, with relief carving, you have to start out like chip carving, but gradually you remove more than simply mere chips. After you end up carving out the initial image you want to relief out of the wood, you have to fine tune it, carve all the curves and carve into the wood for a background. That can be challenging. If done well, however, relief carving can be amazing.

Two dimensional carving is basically any kind of woodcarving done on a two-dimensional surface, such as a flat piece of wood. This can be either chip or relief carving. The difference is that relief carving can give you the illusion of a three-dimensional image.

Three dimensional carving is actually carving a sculpture or figurine out of a block of wood. Three-dimensional carving requires quite a bit of effort and is also very time consuming. Being able to turn a block of wood into an amazing figurine. A very popular form of three dimensional carving is duck decoy carving. You can even get kits on how to carve a duck decoy.

Tools Needed for Woodcarving
To do good quality woodcarving, you will need a specific set of tools. Don't just get the chisels you find at the hardware stores. Those are not woodcarving knives. There is a difference. If you look at a wood chisel, it has a much thicker blade and is designed to be used together with a rubber mallet. When doing intricate carving pieces, those can actually split the wood or ruin your design.

Instead, you should either go to someone who is an avid woodcarver or to a woodcarving store and look for the basic tools you need. You can see what the different tools are below in Figure Two.

Figure Two: Basic tools needed for woodcarving

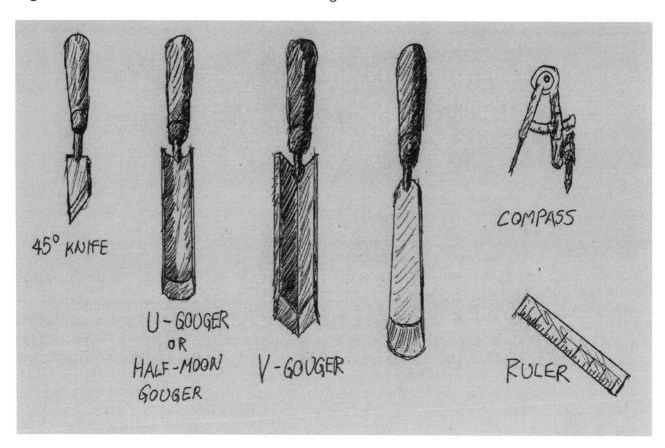

As seen in Figure Two above, there are a wide variety of woodcarving knives you can get and use. The ones portrayed in Figure Two can all be used in both chip and relief carving. Some of them can also be used in three-dimensional carving as well. The tools will be described below.

A. **The 45 degree knife** is your most go-to tool in your woodcarving pieces. This basically looks like an oversized exacto knife. You can get this knife in several different sizes and we recommend that depending on the kind of wood carving you are doing. This knife is used in chip carving to make triangles and squares. The 45 degree knife can also be used for relief and three dimensional carving.
B. **The oval knife** is often used to make half and full ovals in chip carving. This knife has a half oval round edge with one side flat and the other beveled. This is typically used in chip carving and is used to cut the line for the oval and the bevel is used to dig the chip out of the wood.
C. **The half-moon gouger** is an all purpose gouging tool. This can also be purchased in a wide variety of sizes. You can get small ones for small detail and large ones which need a mallet for gouging out bowls and other vessels. Gougers are often used in chip and relief carving. They can also be used in three dimensional carving.
D. **The V-gouger** is also another type of gouger you can add to your arsenal of tools. This is typically used in chip carving and can speed up triangles when making them in a circular fashion.
E. **The lave** is a special tool shown in Figure Three below. The lave is a must have tool for making furniture. The lave is a machine which spins long pieces of wooden post, be they 4X4s or 6X6s. The lave also comes with a series of thick blade knives and gougers which look similar to the above mentioned knives, but on a larger scale. What the lave does is allows you to carve wooden posts, such as bedposts, rail posts for balconies or banisters, and more. The lave will spin the post and with the use of the different knives and gougers, you can create all kinds of ornate decorative beads and nooks to each post.
F. **The Dremel tool** is another handy power tool you can add to your woodcarving arsenal. This neat little device operates on a rechargeable battery and can have all kinds of attachments ranging from small sanding bits to routing bits. This tool can be used to shape the edges of the wood you are carving on and can also be used as a small router and engrave lettering, such as making a wood sign for your front yard or mailbox.
G. **The jigsaw** is a great tool for intricate woodcarving pieces, such as fretting, lattice, or other carved sheets of wood or plywood.

Figure Three: The typical lave and knives which go with it.

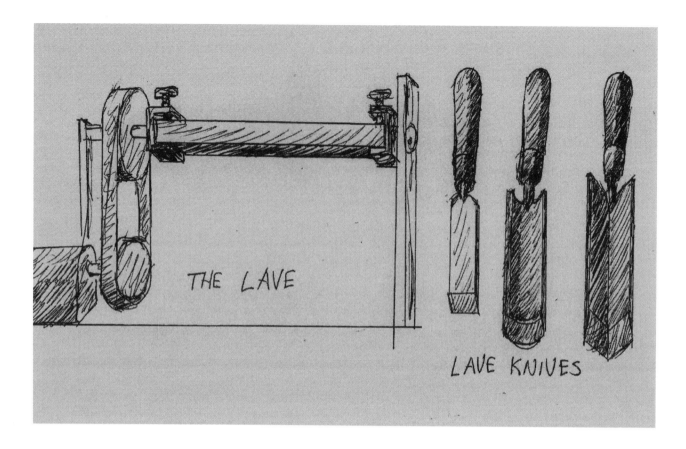

Notice that when working with the lave, you will see that many of the lave knives you will have to work with are much like your larger U-gougers and V-gougers, but one of the lave knives has a square blade, much like an over-sized wood chisel. This particular knife is used to turn a square post, like the one shown above, into a round post.

The Best Carving Woods
You can basically carve on almost any kind of wood, but some woods can be very difficult to work with. In this section we will cover the difference between hard and soft woods, then we will go into different kinds of woods used for woodcarving. Some of the woods can be very difficult to carve and are also very expensive. We will also go into the different grain and color the different woods have and how you can manipulate that in your projects.

Soft woods are the kinds of woods which we recommend you start on when you are doing your first woodcarving project. Most pine varieties, lindens, and like woods are considered soft. This means that the content of the wood has a mass which is easy to cut into. Your knives won't dull as quickly with a soft wood as they would with a hard wood.

Hard woods are woods which are more dense than soft woods. Most of the hard woods include oaks, walnuts, hickory, and other like woods. Some of your more exotic and expensive woods, such as mahogany, teak, and ebony are also considered hard woods.

Varieties of softwoods are readily available at many woodcarving stores, lumberyards, or some large home improvement chains, like Menard's in the Midwest. The best soft woods for carving are listed below.

A. **Bass wood** is a variety of linden tree. This is a very soft wood and is often recommended for beginners because of how easy it is to carve with.
B. **Balsa wood** is a tropical wood which is often used for making model airplanes and gliders, however, you need to be extremely careful when carving balsa wood. Balsa wood is very soft. In fact, balsa wood is so soft that you can even make a mark in it using your fingernail.
C. **Aspen** is a variety of fine grain white pine. Unlike most pines, aspen is a good carving wood, but you need to be very careful when carving in it. With aspen, you want to carve with the grain and use extra care when carving against the grain. Aspen does have a property which most pines have. They tend to chip where you don't want them to when you carve on them. You need to watch for this when carving on aspen. Aspen is harder than the other above mentioned soft woods, so it is ideal for doors, furniture, or other large woodcarving pieces.
D. **Poplar** is also a nice soft wood to work with. Also known as cottonwood, poplar is a soft broad-grain wood. This means that the grain of poplar is highly visible and forms in like a blotchy pattern on the wood. The nice thing about poplar is that it can give you a nice purplish green color.

Varieties of hardwoods are also available. They can be harder to work with than the above mentioned soft woods, but if you have experience carving, you could try your hand at carving on hard woods. Some of the most common and popular hard woods are listed below.

A. **Oak** is one of the most commonly used hardwoods used in the US and around the world. Oak has a wide variety of subspecies ranging from red and white oaks which grow all over the US and Canada, as well as live oaks, which grow in the South. Depending on the variety of oak you use, most oaks have a reddish hue to the wood. Red oaks can have a very red color to them but the white oaks have a lighter red to their wood. Oak is a great wood and is used from making furniture and hardwood floors to picture frames. This is one of the more temperamental hardwoods to work with. Oak has a very coarse grain, thus intricate pieces can break off as you carve them, so use care and try to carve mostly along with the grain when carving oak.
B. **Walnut** is one of the harder hardwoods, but it is the hardwood of choice among accomplished woodcarvers. Walnut has a fine grain and a dark coffee brown color to it. Walnut is very hard to carve and you will have to have your carving knives sharpened several times before finishing your piece.
C. **Mahogany** is also a hardwood, but it is much softer than both walnut and oak. Mahogany is a great wood to work with. Mahogany has a very nice red color to it, even redder than oak.
D. **Cherry** is a very nice hardwood to work with. Cherry wood also has a deep dark red color to it which can be enhanced with stains and give a deep red wine like color. Cherry is also a hardwood which is fairly easy to work with.
E. **Birch** is a wood which has a white color to it and can be a temperamental wood to work with. It does have a fine grain and is nice to work with, however, it does have the hardness of walnut, thus it will dull your knives frequently when working with it.
F. **Ebony** is a hardwood which is imported from Africa. Ebony is very expensive as it is considered an exotic wood. Ebony is famous for its black charcoal color. When carving with ebony, you can create some amazing pieces with a unique color. The neat thing about ebony is that the wood itself is so black that you may think its almost burnt, but it is its natural color. It is a fine and tight grained wood and can be very hard to carve.

G. **Teak** is one of the hardest woods in the world. Imported from southeast Asia, teak has always been the wood of choice for ship and boat building for its hardness. Teak gets its hardness because of silicon crystals which are believed to be growing inside the wood molecules of the tree itself. Thus teak can be very hard to carve and will dull your knives more than oak or walnut. Teak does have a very nice dark red-brownish hue to it which can darken over time. Teak is also often used in making pricy furniture, so it is ideal for making furniture with carved features on it.

You may have to order the more specialty woods, like teak and ebony, but you should first start working with softwoods until you have a feel for the woods and the tools mentioned in this chapter. Once you can carve beautiful pieces on softwoods, then you can try your hand at carving hardwoods. The reason we say that is that hardwoods are much more difficult to carve and can get you frustrated when you do your first carving on it.

Chapter Two

Chip Carving: One of the Oldest and Simplest Forms of Woodcarving

What is chip carving? Well, basically, chip carving is a form of woodcarving which chips of wood are gouged out of the wood to make a geometric design. Typically, geometric designs are very simple to carve into the wood and require few tools. In this chapter you will learn the basics of chip carving. You will learn the following in this chapter.

A. **Choosing your design** which can be tricky for the beginner. You will look at an overview of basic chip carving and see photographs of how intricate designs can be carved using this method. You will also learn how to choose designs from simple to complicated. You will be encouraged to look at books, travel, or look at other resources for ideas both online or at your local library.
B. **Start simple, learn how to cut squares and triangles** which are the simplest forms to carve using the chip carving method. You will learn the basic tools to use and how to use them.
C. **Incorporate circles, semi-circles, and other features** which can be done using some simple U and V gougers.
D. **See how chip carving can be used in your home projects** get ideas from other people's projects. See details of the project photo seen at the beginning.

Choosing your Design
Some of us can be more creative than others. That's natural and there is nothing bad about that. We don't think of you any less if you cannot be as creative as someone else. You have your own gifts as well. You could be very detail oriented, which is also a good thing. You could also be good at copying designs from a book in full detail and using it in your home decor. Others can be extremely creative and see a folk design in chip carving they like and incorporate it or parts of it and create a whole new design. Whatever the case, your level of creativity, you've come to the right place.

What design do you eventually want to create? Is it something that will make a statement or do you just want something to fit the decor of your home or yard. Looking at the photo below, which you've seen in Chapter One also is an idea.

Figure One: Traditional Georgian chip carving design on wooden doors for an outdoor minibar

Take a look at the design on the cabinet door of an outdoor minibar which was designed to emulate ancient Georgian and caucasian culture. Notice how intricate this pattern is. This is all traditional chip carving, which has been an art form in Georgia for centuries. In Russia, Ukraine, and other countries in Europe and Asia have chip carving as a common form of folk art as well.

The idea of this design came from a drawing of a carved leg of an old Georgian table in a book covering different types of Georgian folk art. The artist who built this minibar has traveled to the former Soviet Union, including Georgia, and got ideas for this project. This can be a great way to choose your design also. He simply drew the design on the wood of the door and carved it, chose the right stain and finish and here is the finished project.

You can also find lots of material and images of chip carving online of by going to your local public library. Look for woodcarving guilds or stores also. They'll help you get ideas for good designs.

If you are new to woodcarving, then chip carving is the way to go. It's easy and can help you make simple, yet very intricate designs using simple geometric shapes which you can simply chip out of the wood.

Start Simple: Learning to Carve Triangles and Squares
The easiest shapes to learn in chip carving are squares and triangles. Typically, carving a triangle is very simple. See Figure Two below.

Figure Two: Carving a basic triangle

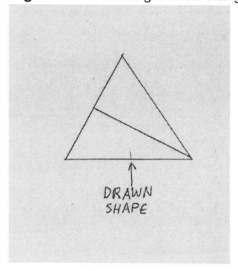
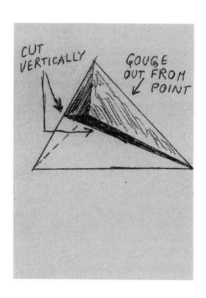

Figure 2a   Figure 2b

To carve a triangle, simply take your 45 degree angle knife and carve as seen on the image above. Simply cut vertically at the part of the triangle you want to have the vertical part on. Notice the drawn shape on Figure 2a. When you draw a triangle, you want to draw a line going from the point to the base. Use this line as a guide when carving out the triangle. When you use your 45 degree angle knife, simply push the point of the knife at the corner of the center line and the base line. The angle of the blade will then make a 45 degree sloped cut vertically in the wood. Then turn the knife around and do the same on the other base line. Then take the knife and cut down vertically along the center line with the point at the base line. If you need to make a shallower angle, then you can simply pivot the knife at the point and the cutting edge will make the right slope from the base to point. Then at the point, Simply position the knife at a 45 degree angle with the point going along the center line. You then get one chip already gouged out as seen in Figure 2b.

Carving a square is basically carving two triangles together. As seen in Figure Three, when drawing a square, you will want to draw two diagonal lines which cross each other in the center.

Figure Three: Carving a basic square.

As you can see in Figure Three, the drawing to the left shows the shape before it's cut. Take your 45 degree knife and place the point in the center where the two diagonal lines meet. Push the knife down on the diagonal lines to have the deepest cut at the intersecting point. If the square is more a rectangle, then simply pivot the knife so the cutting edge makes a vertical cut along each center line. You can then use your V gouger to gouge from corner to the diagonal line. If you have a V gouger, then you only need to cut along only one of the diagonal lines. If you are using the 45 degree angle blade, you might want to draw a horizontal line and a vertical line which intersects the two diagonal lines at the point and carve as you would be carving a triangle.

Note, when carving a triangle, sometimes, using a V gouger can speed up the process and you can have the whole triangle carved out with one gouge.

Incorporate Circles, Semi-Circles, and other Features
Circles are also fairly simple, but they can be complex. You can see how you can actually how different circles can be done. In Figures Four and Five, you can see how complex and how simple you can carve a circle. These photos are details of that Georgian style minibar seen in Figure One.

Figure Four: A complex circular design involving triangles, lines, and half-moons

Notice that in this image, you start by making a series of triangles in a circular fashion with all the points meeting in the center. You also have an outer circle of triangles of different sizes. Then you have lines carved in the wood and half-moon semi-circles gouged in a distinct pattern. You will see how this can be carved below. It starts with a simple circle carving seen in Figure Five below.

Figure Five: A simple circle carved out of a series of triangles

This is the type of circle you need to start with. It is simple to carve with and when you carve the base of the triangles, you can manipulate your 45 degree angle knife to round the bases of the triangle and give it more of a circular shape.

Carving a simple circle is very simple and you already know how to carve a triangle or square. This is basically taking the triangle carving to a new concept. The tools you will need to carve a simple circle with simple triangular formation are as follows:

A. **A compas and pencil** to draw a perfect circle on the wood.
B. **A 45 degree woodcarving knife** to carve along the central and base lines of each triangle. Use the cutting edge of the 45 degree blade to round off the baseline of the triangle. Cut along the center line of each triangle.
C. **A V-gouger (optional)** can simplify the process. Simply use the V-gouger to gouge the point of each triangle to where the baseline was cut. A V-gouger can save you some time when you have many triangles to carve in a circle.

See Figure Six below how a circle should be drawn and carved. The nice thing about using a compass is that, especially in softwoods, the needle will make a small hole in the center vortex of the circle, thus you can have an easier time carving out all the triangles in the circle.

Figure Six: The layout and proper method of carving a simple circle made with triangles.

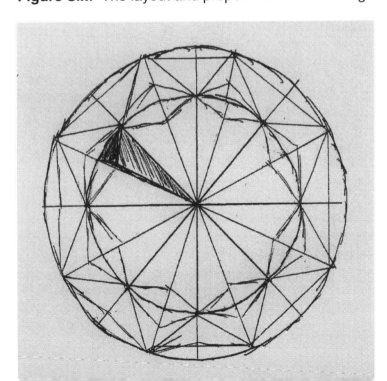

Notice how the circular line made from the compass will be the perfect guide for making the triangles as seen in Figure six. The way this pattern can be drawn on the wood is simple. Use a compass first to draw the two circles. Then make two lines, one horizontal and one vertical which intersect each other at the circle's vortex. The vertical and horizontal lines go all the way to the outer circle. Then draw two diagonal lines which intersect with the two perpendicular lines at the vortex of the circle. The two diagonal lines also go to the outer circle.

Once you have completed this pattern, you will have divided the circle into eight sections. Now, to draw out how the triangles in the inner circle are to be carved, draw the lines dividing each eighth of the circle, but make this line stop at the inner circle. Draw the two diagonal lines which make a point in the lines you have just drawn to determine how shallow or steep of a slope you want the cut to be when you carve out the triangles in the inner part of the circle.

Now, you have the inner parts of the circle drawn out and ready to be carved. Now, it's time to draw out the triangles in the outer circle. Simply extend the lines which stop at the inner circle and you will have a series of 16 squares which you can divide into two triangles by drawing a diagonal line across them. To copy the pattern shown in the above image, you want to make sure that the diagonal lines go in opposing directions. If they went the same direction, you can also get a neat affect. Then draw the lines to cut, like you did for the triangles in the inner circle. Once you're done with that, you're ready to carve.

Using the U-gouger can make a great accent whether you want to make a more complex circle or whether you want to make a fancy line in your design. You will see how to do different patterns at the end of this chapter. The U-gouger has a blade which is shaped like the letter U and has a sharp edge around the whole U edge of the blade.

You can find U-gougers in all kinds of different sizes, but the bigger ones which use the mallet are primarily used for gouging out bowls or other deep divots in the wood you are carving. When using a U-gouger in chip carving, you want to use the smaller U-gougers for half moons and small circles. See Figure Seven to see how to make a half moon.

Figure Seven: Using a small U-gouger to carve half moons.

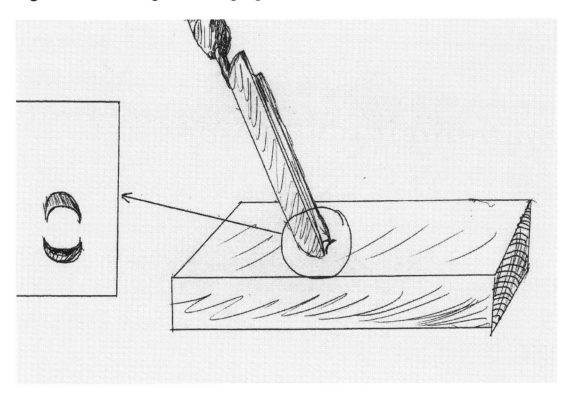

Notice that the U-gouger is a very easy tool to use. To make a simple half moon, simply force the U-gouger into the wood vertically and then go over the round edge and gouge out the U-gouger diagonally and you have your half moon.

Developing designs with half moons can be limitless. You can make squiggly lines, flowers, and many other designs. Incorporate half moons in complex circles, as seen in Figure Four. You can get U-gougers of different sizes to make small and large half moons.

Making small decorative circles can also be done by making two half moons on opposite sides touching each other. You can leave the center in, making a circle out of two half moons or you can gouge the center out and make a small circular divot. You can use this together with half moons to make borders to designs, accents in designs, and more.

Making a complex circle, like the circle you see in Figure Four may look complicated, but it is much easier than you think. Simply start by drawing a simple circle. Widen the compass to make a larger circle outside of the original circle. See Figure Eight below on how to draw the patterns for a more complex circle. Mind you, there are all kinds of different circles you can design and make an impressionable chip carving piece.

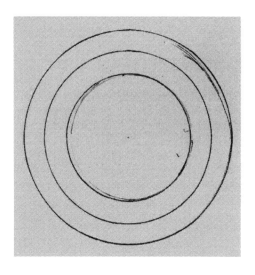
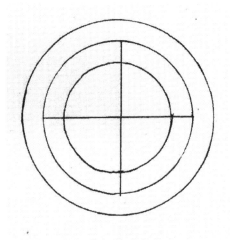

Figure Eight: The steps needed to make a complex circular design in chip carving.

Figure 8a   Figure 8b

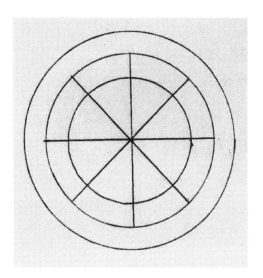
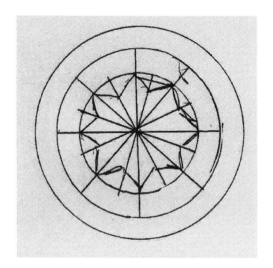

Figure 8c   Figure 8d

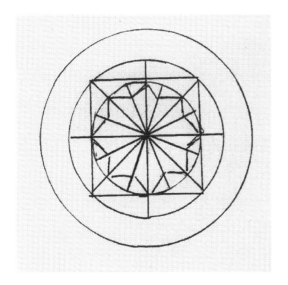
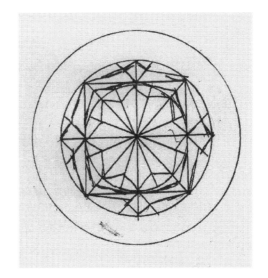

Figure 8e   Figure 8f

Figure 8g

As you notice in Figure 8a, draw the series of circles you want to create the desired effect you want. In Figure Eight, we are showing you the design similar to the one shown in the photograph in Figure Four. This is a fairly complex circular design, with a series of triangles and half moons. There is also some linear carving involved in the outer circles where the half moons are.

On your wood block, after using your compass to draw the series of circles, start drawing the vertical and horizontal lines as seen in Figure 8b. This is just like carving out a simple circle with triangles seen above in Figure Six. Then, as you can see in Figure 8c, you can divide the four quarters in two by drawing two diagonal lines intersecting each other in the center vortex. The vertical and horizontal lines should also intersect each other in the central vortex.

In Figure 8d, you can see that the baselines for the triangles are drawn. Use a ruler or straight edge to draw the straight lines. After drawing the baselines of the triangles, draw a central line to guide you along when you are carving the triangles.

Figure 8e shows you how to do the triangles in the outer rim of the circles can be carved. Simply draw the triangles along the outer circles. This can be repeated as many times you want. Now Figures 8f and 8g can show you how to carve out all the triangles. The other two outer circles we will carve out half moons. The half moons do not need to be drawn. Simply make the outer circles which are to have the half moons, simply make the space between the inner circles and outer circles to be the width of the U-gouger.

To make the circular lines visible, you want to take a very narrow V-gouger or your 45 degree knife and carve a groove along the lines drawn by the compass, however, you want to use care in carving the outer circular lines, as they are to be rather thin, thus they should be done with the finest tool you have in your kit.

Making circles are rather simple when you get the hang of it. Try carving different styles of circles which are simple before attempting to do something very complicated.

Semi-circles are also fairly easy to carve. The are typically carved much like full circles, but in half. Some ideas where semi-circles are shown below in Figures Nine and Ten below.

Figure Nine: Semi-circle at the bottom of a work as part of a greater design.

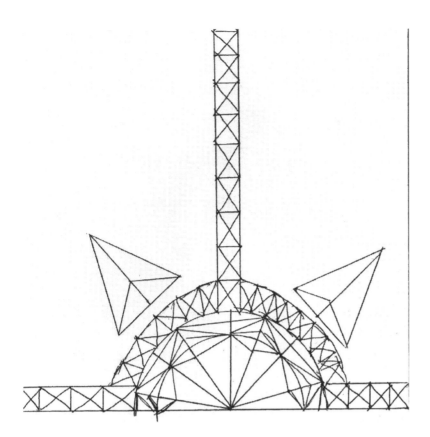

Note that in this image, the semicircle is positioned at the bottom of a work. This can be ornamentation for a desk, cabinet, or other furniture. Basically, carving this pattern is rather simple. All you need to do is the same thing as a circle, then cut the squares by putting the point of your 45 degree angle knife and make the deepest cut in the center of the square and cut from the sides. The triangles then turn into a square with triangular sides which make the deepest point in the middle.

Figure Ten: Semi-circle used under an arched structure in which the carved piece is inserted.

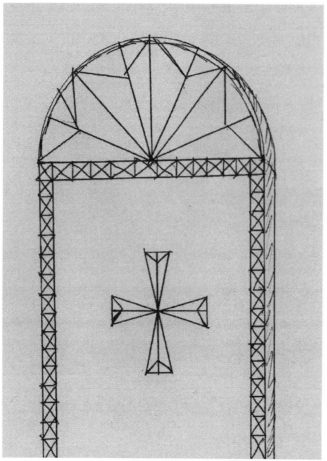

As you notice in the image above in Figure Ten, this can have many possibilities. The four triangles resembling a cross is very common in Georgian woodcarvings on the doors of churches, wooden covers of the Gospel, or other woodcarvings in both churches and homes. As you noticed, the simple semicircle fits into the arched top nicely and the same square pattern adorns the edges on the sides and the top beneath the arch. This can be used on a small scale to make a holder for icons with can fold closed with a locking mechanism, like a traveling pair of icons of the Christ and the Theotokos. This can also be carved on a large scale to be the door to your home, the possibility are endless.

Using the oval knife can make some neat oval shapes. The oval knife is called because of the shape it carves out of the wood, not because of the shape of the blade. As seen in Figure Eleven, the oval knife is very easy to use. Figure 11a, notice that one side of the knife is flat and the other side is beveled. The cutting edge is round. There is a reason for this shape.

Figure Eleven: The oval knife and how to correctly use it.

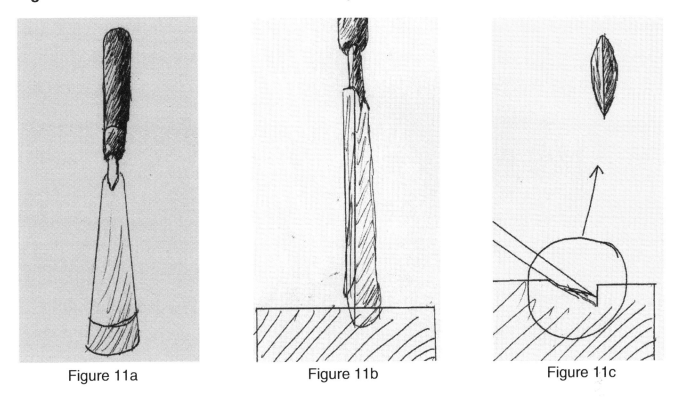

Figure 11a   Figure 11b   Figure 11c

Figures 11b and 11c show how to use the knife to make an oval shaped cut with two sharp corners, kind of like the shape of a football.

Uses for oval cuts in the wood can be many. You can carve oval shapes to make the pedals of flowers with a gouged circle in the center to shape the flower. You can also incorporate oval cuts with triangular cuts to make fancy circle patterns, as seen in Figure 12 below.

Figure Twelve: Complex circle using both oval and triangular cuts.

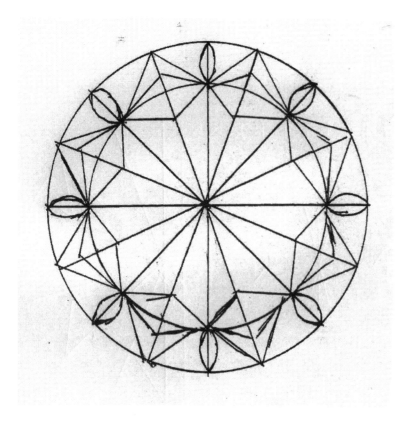

Notice in this circle, you have the triangular action going on in the center as well as in part of the outer circle. The difference here is that the monotony of the triangles are broken with the oval cuts in the circle. Though this is a complex circle and requires some skill to carve, it does have a simple look to it. Triangles are only carved with the points facing outward away from the circle. You can then use a fine carving tool to carve out the line of the outer circle.

Carving an oval can be a bit tricky before you get the hang of it. When carving an oval, you will want to use the cutting edge of the oval and cut vertically into the wood along the center line. Then you carve out each side with the flat side of the knife up. This will gouge out the half of the oval. You will want to do that on the other side of the oval as well.

Incorporating Chip Carving in your Home Projects
Though more intricate chip carving designs can be very time consuming, they are worth taking the time because they can be very beautiful. There is a wide variety of chip carving designs which you can incorporate in your home projects. If you like making furniture, doing cabinets for your kitchen or other parts of your home, or even dressers, hutches, tables, and more, chip carving can make them stand out.

Figure Thirteen: A good idea for a crown design for chip carving. Details from the minibar cabinet doors.

Making chairs can also be a great idea to incorporate chip carving. Typically, when adding chip carving to your chair, the chip carving is usually done on the back support of the chair. You can do this with a combination with other woodcarving, including laves, see Chapter Six.

Wooden boxes for small items, such as jewelry, coins, precious stones, relics, or other important items are often very nice with ornamentation in chip carving. This has been a tradition in many eastern European cultures which wood boxes have always been used in gift giving or keeping small valuables. If you can use chip carving and make small boxes for gifts to someone important in your life, you can make a memorable gift which that person can cherish for years to come. A gift which is a work of your own hands is a great thing to give, as it is uniquely from you.

Moldings and wooden accents affixed to permanent structures in your home are also ideal for chip carving. Chip carving your own molding can be very time consuming, especially if it is a large room, but it is very beautiful. Typically, if you want to incorporate chip carving in molding, you want to do it on your crown molding, which is the molding which goes along the parameter of the ceiling.

Chip carving is also great for parts of your trim around your doors and windows. Use wood squares around the corners of your trim versus cutting your trim at a 45 degree angle using a miter saw. You can make all kinds of patters from circles to other shapes on the corner squares. When making corner squares with chip carving on them, you want to make the corner squares a bit wider than your trim.

Other designs you can incorporate in your chip carving design are limitless. One thing you can develop is your own style. By looking at books, and resources online, you can get many different ideas. Let's look at the Georgian minibar again. You can create unique images, such as this image of a person, as seen in Figure Fourteen below.

Figure Fourteen: Design of a man using chip carving. This is influenced from an ancient Georgian folk design.

Note that this image of a man is surrounded by an intricate design and this figure of a man is on both cabinet doors. The original Georgian design which this pattern is influenced by was from the leg of a table. It was incorporated into the design for the cabinet doors of the minibar to fit with the Georgian motif.

Seeing some more details which this design was created, intersecting triangular lines, which are shown below in Figure Fifteen.

Figure Fifteen: Cross lines carved out of a series of triangles.

The person who did this chip carving design simply learned for two years and was able to create a work of this kind of stature. One of the greatest things about chip carving is that it is easy to learn and you can just let your imagination go wild.

Chapter Three

Relief Carving

Now that you have mastered chip carving, you can try your hand at relief carving. What exactly is relief carving? Well, basically, relief carving is a form of three dimensional carving on a two dimensional plane. Where chip carving is simply carving chips out of the wood to create a design. Basically, relief carving is chip carving on steroids.

The Difference Between Chip and Relief Carving

Basically, chip carving is the stepping stone to relief carving. Chip carving is basically the creation of geometric patterns on the wood whereas relief carving can be more. Out of relief carving, you can create patterns involving foliage, fruits, images of human and animal figures, and more.

The basic relief carving design begins with carving chips out of the wood, like you would be doing a chip carving but a bit more complex. The basic steps are covered below.

A. **Start simple** when undertaking your first relief carving. Do something like grapes with leaves. This is simple enough and you can start by doing your basic chip carving. Simply see Figures 1a to 1f. Start by drawing the image of the grape leaves and fruits.
B. **After drawing image, start carving chips out between the grapes.** You will want to use your 45 degree knife and carve triangles and squares between the grapes and leaves. Carve as you learned in Chapter Two about chip carving. This allows you to already see the shapes of the leaves and grapes. The only different thing you need to do is to have a more vertical cut near the grapes and leaves.
C. **Round off the grapes** by carefully carving off the sharp corners using a 45 degree knife or using a fine U-gouger. You can also use a U-gouger to carve out the larger spaces between the leaves and edges.
D. **Carve out the texture of the grape leaves** by using many of the different techniques you learned in Chapter Two when chip carving.

You can also combine chip carving with relief carving, by carving out a folk pattern around the relief carving. See Figure One below.

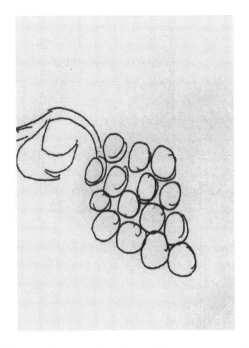 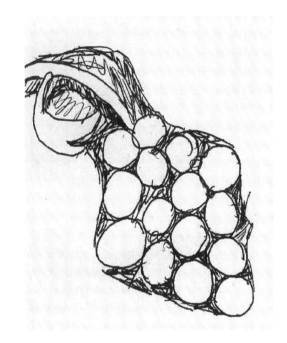

Figure One: See the different steps in carving a grape vine pattern.

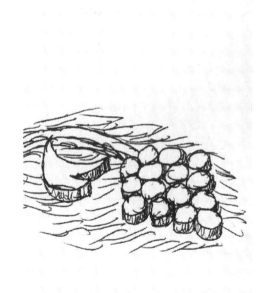 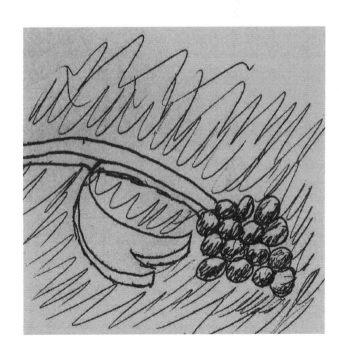

Figure 1a: Drawing of design on the wood

Figure 1b: Carving out chips

Figure 1c: Basic form of grapes and vine

Figure 1d: Rounding the grapes

Figure 1e: Carving texture on leaves   Figure 1f: Finished product

A grape vine is a fairly simple carving to do and is a great accent piece for moldings, accents around windows and cabinets, and more. The grapevine pattern is seen in many ancient cultures, especially those which are known for producing wine.

Common simple relief carvings include grapes and leaves, round fruits, flowers, animals, primarily birds. As seen in the drawings with Figure One, a grape motif is a more simple type of relief carving, thus we recommend doing that is easier than carving a whole image of a human figure.

Tools needed for relief carving include all the tools mentioned in Chapter Two for chip carving. The difference is that you tend to be using less of the V-gouger and more of the U-gouger. How the tools are used differs from chip carving.

Your 45 degree knife is your basic tool for relief carving. This is the tool which you will be using to do most of your carving. The 45 degree knife can be used to begin carving out the areas around the shapes of the image which will make the brunt of your relief.

When carving the basic image of your relief carving, you want to make sure that your 45 degree knife will be making more vertical cuts around the shapes of the images. Sometimes, you can also use your 45 degree knife to carefully gouge out areas where there is supposed to be open space. If the areas of open space are rather wide, then you should use your U-gouger to carve out the area. The U-gouger can also be used to make for interesting background texture in the open space.

Carving the objects which are the relief can be done with the combination of your 45 degree knife and small U-gougers. You want to use care in carving the relief shapes, as not to cut too much wood off at once. This can ruin the work and that kind of mistake can be very difficult to eliminate.

The basic tip for carving out the texture of the relief shapes is to simply start around the top of the corner. Using your 45 degree knife, carefully carve around the sharp corner which is made by gouging out the open space between the shapes. See Figure Two for details.

Figure Two: See how you can use your 45 degree knife for shaping shapes.

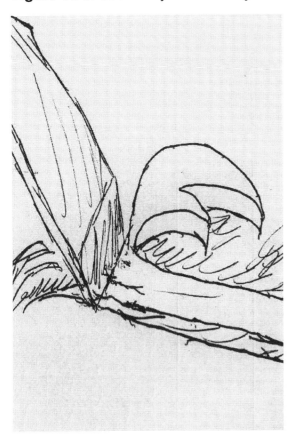

When using the 45 degree knife to shape the reliefs you are carving, you should use extra care and shave off as little wood at a time. This part of relief carving does take a lot of patients and any rush job could ruin the work.

Use of the U-gouger can be more frequent in relief carving. The U-gouger is a versatile tool and can be used for adding texture in the open spaces for background. You can use the U-gouger to also round corners, create the impression of water, and more.

Care should be using the U-gouger, as the U-shape of its blade can easily gouge too deeply. Check with your local hobby or art supply store which has woodcarving supplies. You want to have several different U-gougers. Some are very fine and can be used to gouge out small spaces, whereas others are big enough to need a mallet to use. Relief carving pays attention to some of the finest details, thus you will want a series of fine U-gougers for carving into the smaller nooks and crannies of your work. In some cases, you might even need a V-gouger to do some of the work.
The V-gouger is a special tool which gouges out the wood, like the U-gouger, gouges out wood. The difference is that the V-gouger has a V-shaped blade, thus is designed to gouge out

a V-shape trench in the wood. Like U-gougers, the V-gouger comes in different sizes and when it comes to relief carving, the smaller the better.

Sometimes, you can actually use the V-gouger and the 45 degree knife simultaneously to carve out more complicated parts of your relief carving.

More Complex Relief Carving
Once you have mastered the simpler relief carving motifs, such as grapes, fruits, foliage, and berries, you can try a more difficult image, animals, people, etc. What makes relief carving stand out from basic chip carving is how more creative you can be with it. It is more complicated than chip carving and more difficult to learn, but once you have mastered the simplest designs like the ones shown above, you can create almost anything on a two dimensional image. Let's look at a more complex image below.

Figure Three: The carving of a bird

If you notice the type of bird which is shown in Figure Three, it is a rather difficult image to carve out and make a relief image with some three dimensional feel to it. What you need to do first is to carve out the spaces around the bird. This will be your background on the piece of wood. You want to make sure that your block of wood which you are carving on is deep enough to give good depth in the background. This is especially key if you want things in your background, like trees, hills, or water.

The key to image depth in relief carving is to have the foreground first at the level from start, the background at mid level, and then the far background being gouged out with a U-gouger. See Figure Four below where the bird and the trees in the background are being carved out. Notice in Figure 4a, that after the shapes are initially carved out, now, notice in Figure 4b, the bird is more close up and the trees are carved lower with the sky or water being gouged out with a narrow U-gouger.

Figure Four: Carving out the bird and the trees in the background
          Figure 4a   Figure 4b

Note that when you see the artist carving the image in Figure 4a is the basic shape of the bird and the trees. Now notice that in figure 4b, the trees are being carved into shape and the bird is slowly being worked on. There is a reason for this. The trees are supposed to be lower in the wood, whereas the bird is right at the top. If the trees have leaves, you will want to use the U-gouger for adding the leaves on the branches before gouging out the filler in the background.

Carving the detail in the foreground should have the last priority. The reason is that you need to carve down in the wood. Once you have the shapes carved out, you will want to first roughly gouge out the background between all the shapes. You will want to gouge the spaces out deep enough so you can have different areas of height throughout the entire piece. You then carve out parts of the foreground to determine its height and you work on the background. Then you carve the near background, in this case, the trees.

Figure Five: The finished product

If you notice that with the finished product, you can see that the bird is clearly in the foreground. Once you have finished the near background and the foreground, it's time to decide what type of texture you want to give your far background.

The most common tool for gouging out the background of a relief piece, is the U-gouger. You can also use the V-gouger, but that will give some sharp lines. The V-gouger can be great for creating a horizon with a sea or lake in the image. Using the V-gouger and the U-gouger can create a wavy pattern to give the feel of a large body of water.

Other gougers used in relief carving are also available, though they are not as common as the U-gouger and V-gouger. One gouger has a trough shape which allows for a wider and smoother background.

Where Can Relief Carving be Introduced in your Home?
Well, there is a variety of things you can do once you have sharpened your relief carving skills. You can use more simple patters and carve them on longer pieces of trim and molding to use as accents and decoration around windows and doors, crown moldings, etc. Doing a molding or trim in relief carving, however, can take forever.

Furniture is ideal for displaying your relief carving. Carve out the cabinet doors, accents on frames of glass doors for your dining room hutch, add accents to your table legs and on the backs of chairs.

Pictures and icons can also be carved in relief on a block of wood. Sometimes it can be a very nice thing for you to have on your walls, especially if you have wood and natural stone features as accents in your home.

Relief carving is one of the more difficult forms of woodcarving, but you can get more detailed and develop your two dimensional woodcarving. Using relief carving and chip carving together can also create some awesome designs on wood.

Chapter Four

Two Dimensional Woodcarving

What is two dimensional woodcarving? Basically, two dimensional woodcarving is woodcarving which is flat on one plane. Basically, two dimensional woodcarving is the type of woodcarving you have learned in the past two chapters for both chip and relief carving. Basically, this chapter will deal with what you do with two dimensional woodcarving.

Pictures to hang on the wall is the most common use of two dimensional woodcarving. Typically, relief carving is used in two dimensional woodcarving for pictures to hang on the wall. Typically, this is an art developed by eastern Europeans, primarily as religious art among some of the Roman Catholic Slav and Indo-European countries, such as Poland and Lithuania, and many of the eastern European countries which have the Orthodox Christian faith, like Russia, Ukraine, Romania, Serbia, Greece, Georgia, and others. The religious imagery typically includes relief carved crucifixes, icons, and other like artwork. In some cases, Lithuanian woodcarvings can also have amber stones engraved or glued to them.

Facades on furniture are also common with two dimensional woodcarving. Two dimensional woodcarvings include images of birds and other animals or people, flowers, and fruits in a motif on cabinet doors, head boards for beds, jewelry boxes, and other items.

Crosses and pendants are very common in eastern European countries. In many cases, the wood cross pendants for Orthodox priests are made for Lent and other fasting seasons. The crucifixes which are worn by priests can be ornately carved with a two dimensional relief carving. Some Roman Catholic cultures also carve wooden crosses and pendants, which are much simpler. Both Catholics and Orthodox will also carve two dimensional crosses for the lay people to wear. Typically, wood used for making these kinds of pendants are either olive or walnut.

Doing two dimensional woodcarving is very easy and if you are already capable of doing chip carving and relief carving, then you are literally doing two dimensional woodcarving. In the next chapter we will cover three dimensional woodcarving, which is much more complicated and more difficult.

Chapter Five

Three Dimensional Woodcarving

You are now about to learn to do the most difficult and involved form of woodcarving there is. Three dimensional woodcarving can involve both chip and relief carving, depending on what you are carving, but it goes much deeper. In this chapter you will learn all the deep aspects of woodcarving, such as the following:

A. **Carving bowls and utensils** which is the basic in three dimensional woodcarving. There are many reasons why you should start with carving bowls and utensils when first learning three dimensional woodcarving. Wood bowls are very beautiful and can be used as vessels for candy, decorative pieces, etc. Carving large spoons are also great for wall decorations. Once you have learned how to carve a bowl out of wood, you can then take it up a notch and learn how to make musical instruments, such as lutes and mandolins.
B. **Carving figurines** is the most intricate aspect of three dimensional woodcarving. Carving figurines is very delicate and can be used from everything to making dolls all the way to making carvings of Mary, Jesus, and saints for statues or prayer corners.
C. **Carving duck decoys** may be simpler than carving complicated figurines, but these are also complicated. You will learn how to carve out the shape of a duck or other type of bird out of two blocks of wood.

Prior to learning the above things, you will also learn about the best woods to use when undertaking three dimensional carving. As mentioned before, woods play a key role in how your work will turn out. You have hard and soft woods which can play a huge role on how quickly or slowly you can carve out your three dimensional piece. You need to understand that when doing three dimensional carving, you are carving off more wood than when you are doing any form of two dimensional carving, be it chip carving or relief carving.

Basswood or linden wood is the best kind of wood for people who are starting out. Basswood and linden wood are the same wood. This is a white wood, but it is also a softwood. This is a wood which is easy to carve and when using a large U-gouger with a mallet, you will have an easy time to gouge out the areas you need to hollow out.

Other woods, such as walnut, are hardwoods and are great if you want to carve out a salad bowl, but they are extremely difficult to carve, especially for beginners. We recommend that you practice first with basswood before you do three dimensional carving with hardwoods. We don't recommend using soft woods for carving salad bowls because of the woods being more porous than hardwoods, but if your desire is to make salad bowls, practice by making decorative bowls out of basswood first.

Carving Bowls and Utensils
Carving bowls and utensils out of wood is the best way to start learning three dimensional woodcarving. The reason for this is that this is basic and you learn how to shape the wood, hollow it out and all the other things you will need to know how to do when carving more complicated pieces, such as musical instruments, figurines, and other three dimensional items.

If you want to learn woodcarving for musical instruments, then learning how to carve bowls and utensils is a prerequisite, as the sound boxes of most string instruments are a carved out wooden bowl.

Carving your basic wood bowl is simple, at first, but if you don't do it correctly, you can ruin the whole project. Try not to gouge out the bowl first. Before you carve, however, you want to learn about the tools you will need to carve out a wooden bowl. These instruments are listed below.

A. **The U-gouger** is the instrument which you will be using most of the time to do most of your carving. As mentioned before, there are different sizes of U-gougers, but when it comes to making carving out bowls, you will want to get a couple of large U-gougers and a rubber mallet. If you want to make a rectangular bowl or a box, you might also want to consider getting a 90 degree V-gouger to gouge out the corners.
B. **The V-gouger** is needed if you have sharp corners which you want to carve out sharper corners. Typically, you will want to get a 90 degree V-gouger versus the 45 degree V-gouger used in chip and relief carving.
C. **Fine-tooth saw** can sometimes be used to carve off larger corners. There are different types of fine tooth saws available. One is the hand bandsaw, which has a thick metal handle with a thin saw band which is tightly attached to the metal structure. (See Figure One) The other fine tooth saw is used as a hand miter saw without the miter box. This is a stronger saw blade and is great for cutting off large parts of wooden corners. (See Figure Two)
D. **Corse and fine grit sandpaper** to finish off the bowl and create a smooth finished surface ready for either oiling or varnishing.

Figure One: Fine tooth hand band saw

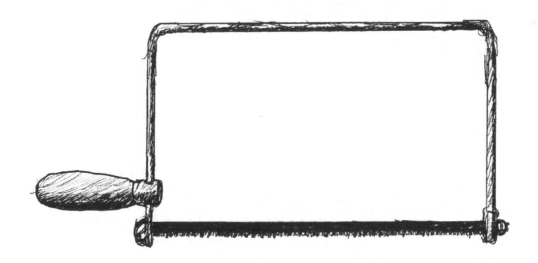

Figure Two: Fine tooth solid blade saw, hand miter saw without box

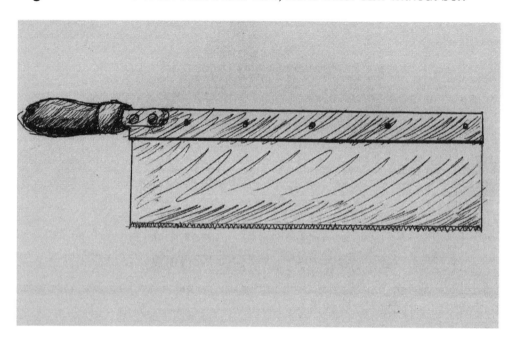

Choosing your wood block for your bowl can also be tricky. When making a good quality strong solid bowl, you want to choose a good wood block which has fine grains and little or no knots.

Problems with knots in wood are various. First problem is that where you find a knot in the wood, carving that area can be difficult as that area is much harder than the rest of the wood. Knots form in the wood where a branch grows out. This basically doubles the density of the wood, thus it is harder. In other cases, a knot can also create a hole in the wood as the branch is a wood of its own and can sometimes cause the main wood of the trunk grow around it.

Size of wood block also matters when looking to carve a wood bowl. Depending on the size of the wood bowl you want to carve out, you have to choose a block of significant size. This can sometimes be hard to find. Many woodcarving shops will sell carving quality woods, such as basswood, but sometimes, you might have to go to the lumberyard to get a big enough block.

When choosing your block, you want to make sure that your block is solid and not glued together with smaller blocks of wood to make a bigger block. To carve a basic size bowl, for example, a cereal bowl, you may want to get a wood block that is a cubic foot. That is each face of the block is 12 inches by 12 inches. If you are a beginner and this is the first bowl you are carving, you might want to find a block larger than that.

Carving out the basic shape of the bowl is done by first drawing out a circle in the area where you want to gouge out your bowl. You will want to then draw diagonal lines at the corners where you want to cut off the excess wood. (See Figure Three.)

Figure Three: Wood block with the circular marking for gouging and diagonal lines for removal of excess wood

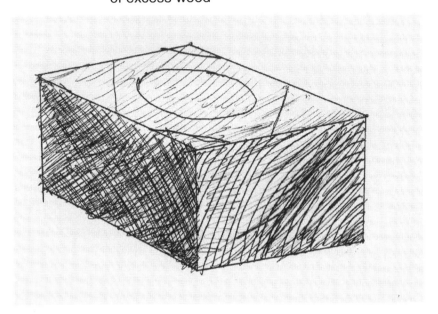

After marking your block, you will want to take your fine tooth saw and cut off the corners. You may want to get some large vice clamps to hold the block to the workbench when cutting the corners.

Depending on the block, you might want to use the solid blade miter saw to cut the corners off first. You will be cutting a large volume of wood off the corners. Make sure you have some space between the circle which you plan to gouge out and the corners. As you cut off the corners, you can use the delicate saw to cut parts of the wood off the new corners to make the sides more round. You only want to cut vertically and not cut into the bottom. You will do this later, after you have gouged out the center.

When finished cutting out the corners of your block, you will be ready to gouge out the interior of your bowl. Your block should look something like you see in Figure Four below.

Figure Four: Notice how block has a rough shape of the top of the bowl.

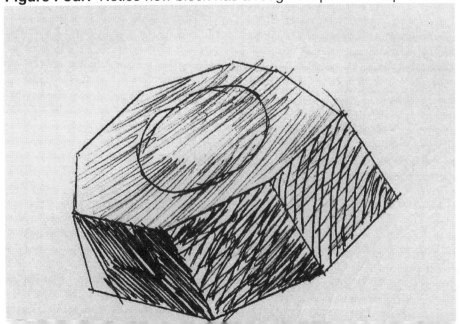

Notice how the block was cut to get close to the bowl's shape. Once you have used your saws to cut the corners off, you will be ready to gouge out the interior of the bowl.

Creating a fence vice is a good idea before you begin to gouge out the interior of the bowl. You cannot really find a fence vice at any lumberyard, home improvement store, or woodcarving shop. This is something you have to make yourself. A fence vice is easy to make. Get a couple of pipe clamps and two pieces of 2X12s or 2X8s. You want to make sure the 2X12s or 2X8s are long enough to keep manageable and you want to have enough room to hold the block and keep it from moving while you are gouging out the center for your bowl. Simply place the block in the center of the two 2X12s and clamp the two pipe clamps tightly to prevent your block from moving. You may want to screw pieces of 1X2s to the 2X12s as an extra precaution in preventing the pounding of the mallet from dislodging the block from the make-shift vice. See Figure Five below.

Figure Five: The fence vice

Notice this is an image of an old fashioned fence vice. It's called a fence vice because the two plates work like fences and this type of vice is designed to hold large wood blocks to keep them from moving. If you can't find a fence vice, you can easily create one by using some strong boards and a couple of large pipe clamps. We recommend using two 2X4s nailed together or two 4X4s to use for the fences. Place the wood block between both of them and clamp down tightly with the pipe clamps.

Gouging out your bowl's interior is one of the most difficult phases of the project. You want to be gentle and do not gouge too deeply. Hold the large U-gouger at a shallow angle and gently tap with the rubber mallet. Making the angle too deep can cause the block to split and then you may have a crack in your finished bowl or even worse, you may have to start all over again.

You want to begin to gouge out the center of your bowl from the center of the circle. When drawing your circle before even cutting the block, you may want to consider using a compass, and use the point in the wood made from the compass needle. This is the exact center of the circle. You want to start gouging at the center of that circle. Simply hold the U-gouger and tap with the mallet until you see wood shavings come out. With each tap, you will notice the hole getting bigger. You will want to get the hole gouged out until it is about half the depth of the entire block. See Figure Six below.

Figure Six: See how the hole should be carved out of the wood.

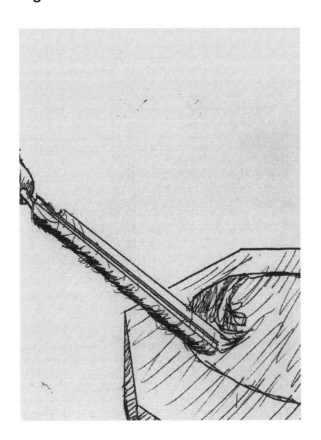

Figure 6a

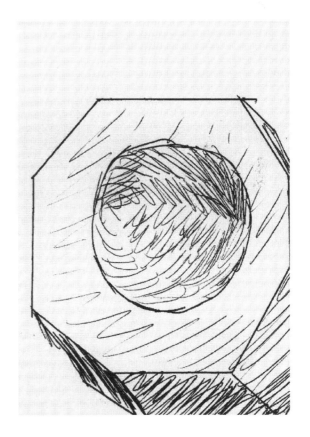

Figure 6b

Notice that in Figure 5a, you can see the gouged out interior of the bowl. It's still corse, but you will sand it later. Figure 5b shows you the block and shows the depth of how the interior of the bowl should be carved.

Carving the exterior of the bowl is very tricky. You want part of the bottom to be flat so the bowl can stand by itself unless you are making it for a musical instrument. Musical instruments will be briefly covered in this chapter after learning how to carve the basic bowl and utensils. You want to take the delicate band saw and gently cut all the corners at the bottom of the block until the block looks faceted, like a large diamond cut. See Figure Seven below.

Figure Seven: The prep cut for bowl

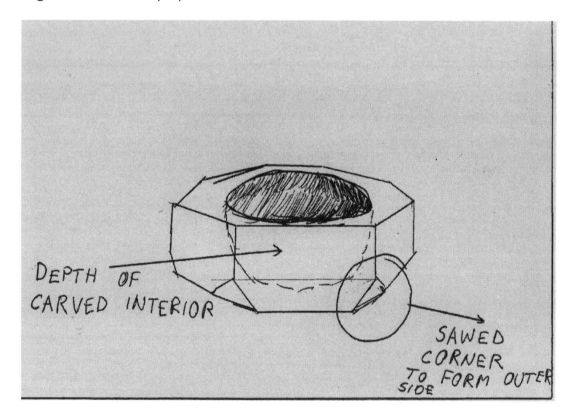

Notice how here, you can use the hand band saw to cut the bottoms of the corners of the bottom of the bowl. The dotted line in the image indicates how deep the interior of your bowl should be gouged out. You may need to delicately cut off corners and get a rough shape of the outside of the bowl and make sure the bowl's walls are at their proper thickness or as close to the desired thickness as possible. Cut thin layers off with the hand band saw.

Smoothing out the cut corners of your bowl is first done with the largest U-gouger you can use by hand. This work will be too delicate to use a rubber mallet, so you will want to carve this slowly by hand. Carve first on the sharp corners and then gently carve away all which makes the block look like a block. During this part of the process, you should be able to see the wood block beginning to look more like a bowl.

After having carved out your bowl, and it already has the shape you want it to have, it's time to sand it down.

Sanding your bowl can take some time, as you might not be able to use a power sander to do it. You're much better off using a piece of sandpaper to sand until smooth.

The proper way to sand your finished bowl is to start with a course grit sandpaper. This will help you get all the corse edges and ridges caused by the gougers smoothed down. Once you have seen that the surface is smooth, use a fine grit sandpaper to fine tune the surface and then the bowl is ready for finishing.

Finishing your bowl depends on what you want to use it for. There are many kinds of finishes out there, and we do have all of Chapter Seven dedicated to that. When planning to use your wooden bowl for serving food, we do not recommend using varnishes or shellacks to finish your bowls, as these do contain some toxic substances which can leach into your food. Instead, you want to use some natural oil, such as olive oil or other plant oil commonly used in cooking. The wood will absorb the oils and the oils will help preserve it. It may feel oily at first, but the key is to rub the oil into the wood and eventually it will become dry to the touch.

Carving out utensils, such as wooden spoons or ladles is similar to carving out your bowl. You may have to cut more out of your initial wood block to fashion the shape of a ladle, but making a spoon or ladle is much like carving out the bowl but with a handle attached to it. The only difference is that you will need to carve out the bowl part of the spoon or ladle with a smaller U-gouger and not use a mallet. Using a mallet can break the spoon, as it is a more delicate piece.

Creating musical instruments can also be done once you have learned how to carve your basic wooden bowl. Making your own musical instrument, which is unique to you as your own creation has often been a dream of many experienced musicians and by altering the shape of your wooden bowl, you can create the sound box of many different kinds of wooden instruments. Typically, most wooden string instruments which use the wooden sound box carved out of a wooden bowl include lutes. The lute is a common string instrument used in many cultures. Some variations of a lute include the oud, played in all the Middle Eastern countries, Turkey, and Armenia, the panduri and chonguri, played in Georgia, the mandolin, played in southern Europe, the Bazuki, played in Greece, and other similar instruments. You can determine the pitch of the sound by how big or how small you make your sound box. The bigger the sound box, the lower the tones and pitch, the smaller the sound box, the higher the tones and pitch. For example, you want a deep base sound, you will have to get a fairly large block of wood to carve out the bowl.

When carving out the sound box for your instrument, you will want to make room for a type of spoon handle, so you can securely attach the fret board and other aspects you will need for a string instrument. You will also have to find some thin plywood of fine quality to cover the top of the bowl to effectively make the sound box work.

Carving Figurines

Once you have mastered carving out your wooden bowl, the next thing you need to learn is how to carve figurines. Carving figurines is a fairly complicated aspect of three dimensional woodcarving.

What exactly are figurines? Figurines are miniature statues of people or animals which can be arranged in a particular setting, such as Christmas decorations, shadow boxes, and other themes. Typically, in America and Europe, the most popular motif for carving figurines among most hobbyists are for a Christmas setting. Sometimes you can even add additional skills, such as relief carving to make houses according to the size of the figurines you are carving to create a nativity scene, or a village scene.

When carving your basic figurine, you will need a wood block which is at least twice the size of the figurine you plan to carve. Like with anything else, you want to start simple and then go on to more complicated figurines as you become proficient at carving wooden figurines.

You want to sketch the basic shape of the figurine you want to carve on the block of wood and then begin carving using your saws and 45 degree knife. See Figures Eight through Ten to see how to properly carve out the basic shape of the figurine.

Figure Eight: The image of a dog on the block

Notice that in this image, you can see the basic image of the dog. You will want to trace the image on tracing paper and then cut out the same shape on the other side of the block. As you see below in Figure Nine, you can see how the block looks like when you have carved the initial two dimensional shape of the dog.

Figure Nine: The basic two dimensional shape of the dog.

As you see above in Figure Nine, You now have the basic two dimensional shape and all the features of the dog, the paws, ears, and head are all carved out as ridges on the block. Here is where the real challenges begin. Once you have reached this shape, you will need to go ahead and start gently cutting the space between the dog's paws, areas where the tail is supposed to be, and begin to carve the shape. You can use the hand band saw for this, but you want to make sure you have a good set of bench vices to hold the work in when you get to this stage. A bench vice is the vice which you can bolt to your workbench.

Figure Ten: Notice how the dog is now ready for the second phase of carving

As seen above in Figure Ten, you can see that now you have the basic shape of the dog and you can go ahead and start shaping out the dog. Start with the head by carving out the space on top between the ears and then begin by carving out the snout. As you start carving out the snout, you will notice the whole head of the dog beginning to take shape.

From the head you can also start carving the body and work your way to the tail. Simply start carving the top of the body and round off the top of the body and you can see the whole dog begin to take shape. As you begin to carve the tail, you will already have the whole top of the dog shaped as seen below in Figure Eleven.

Figure Eleven: See how the top of the dog and its tail has already been shaped

After having gotten as far as seen above, you can now begin to carve out the paws of the dog. Start with carving between the paws and you can then see how the paws should be shaped as proportioned to the body. You can then carve out the shape of the paws and the bottom part of the body. By that time, you will have the finished product as seen below in Figure Twelve.

Figure Twelve: The finished product

Though this drawing may not do it justice, this is supposed to be a dog carved from the wood block shown above.

A dog or cat is probably the simplest form to start with when working on a figurine. Carving human figures can be more complicated, but with some more experience it can be done. After carving the dog, you can then start sanding the figurine and begin to paint it.

Sanding the figurine of the dog is done much like sanding the bowl. You need some corse grit and fine grit sandpaper and sand first with the corse grit and then with the fine grit.

Painting to make the figurines look real, you will have to choose different paints. Chapter Seven will go deeper in different finishes, such as stains and varnishes, but painting of figurines is special and will be covered here. Basically, there are all kinds of paints on the market for wood, but you might need a primer before you can paint your figurine.

Primers are a special chemical which is applied to the raw wood surface which can adhere to the wood and also to the paint. Many different paints will need a primer to be painted onto the wood before the paints can be applied.

Advice on carving human figurines can be complex, but we advise you to start with simpler figurines, such as animals before you start carving human figures. Carve animals which are easy to shape, such as dogs, cats, bears, pigs, etc. The thing about carving human figurines, you will have to learn how to carve creases in clothing, facial features, etc.

Tools needed for carving figurines are many. Figurines are such a fine work of woodcarving, you will need to have a wide assortment of tools and gougers with very fine blades. You need to have some of the smallest gougers possible and even get some special needle tools which have small elliptical blades to carve some of the finer lines of your figurine. Judging the types of fine tools you need, we recommend that for beginners, you should use a good fine grain softwood, such as basswood. The primary tools needed to carve figurines are listed below.

A. **The 45 degree knife** is the staple knife for any woodcarving project. This is a versatile carving knife which you can use to gouge out triangles and also carving away excess wood from the initial block.
B. **U-gougers** from medium to small sizes. U-gougers are used to gouge out nooks and crannies of the figurine you are carving out. Some of the smaller details need a small gouger, thus fine U-gougers can be used for smaller details, such as carving out the space between ears and legs for animal figurines, such as dogs and cats.
C. **V-gougers** are needed, but in the smallest sizes. In animal figurines, the small V-gougers can be used to carve out the lines between the claws of the animal's paws or in carving out some scaling, which you would find on birds legs or reptiles. In human figurines, the small V gougers can be used in carving out the lines for the larger pleats in clothing, lines between fingers and toes (if the figurine is barefoot). The small V-gougers can also be used in carving out some of the larger facial features on your figurine.
D. **Elliptical carving needles** are large needle like tools, but they do not have a handle. Some carving needles have a different blade on both ends, be careful not to cut yourself with

those. The elliptical carving needle tip is actually specifically designed to carve small holes in your figurine, such as eyes, nostrils, the opening of the mouth between lips.
E. **Curved carving needles** have a fish hook shape and are often used for fine gouging of rounded surfaces, such as heads, bodies of animals, legs, arms, hands, and feet. The curved carving needles have a sharp edge on the fish hook part of the needle.

Figure Thirteen: The tools needed for figurine carving

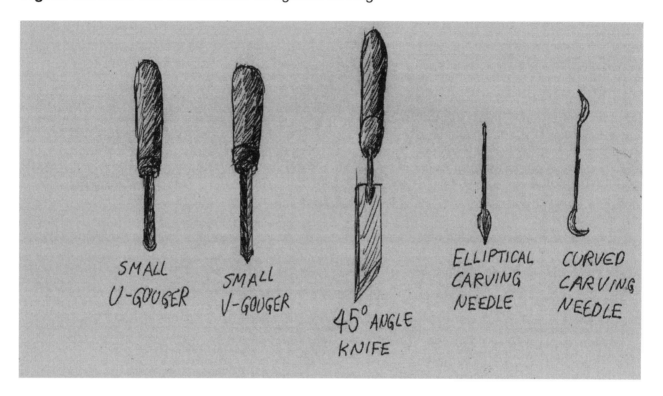

Carving Duck Decoys

Carving duck decoys out of wood has become a very popular past time. Also known as bird carving, carving duck decoys has been an age old art form and has also been quite useful in the times when people would be hunting ducks for food. Typically, duck decoys are painted in great detail of the breed of duck or goose it is aimed to attract to the hunters.

Buying duck decoy kits can be done at Hobby Lobby, or any other hobby shop which sells woodcarving supplies for beginners. Basically, duck decoy kits can be sold as collectibles and some will even have the right size wood block for carving with the image on it. Typically, wooden duck decoys are made to float on water to attract the female ducks to the kill site, so they are often painted as colors of mallards and are carved from a light wood, such as balsa or basswood. A word to the wise about balsa wood, however. Balsa is not only very light and floats, but it also is a very soft wood. In fact balsa wood is so soft that you can even make a mark in the wood with your fingernail.

Duck decoys today are primarily made to add an outdoorsy feel to your home and are often used to accent the lodge or cottage at the lake or in the mountains. Duck decoys look good on shelves where you have a couple of deer heads mounted on the wall and other outdoor themed nicknacks in your home.

Carving a duck decoy from scratch is a bit more of a challenge than making one from a kit, but our advice is that if you want the decoy to be as close to the real thing as possible, you will want to get a nature guide with accurate drawings or photos of different species of ducks to get ideas. Carve accordingly.

Getting started on your decoy, is quite simple. Simply get a large rectangular block to carve out the body and a smaller rectangular or square block to carve out the head. This will be much easier for you to carve than carving the entire decoy out of one block. The trick is that you will need to carve the decoy's body and head simultaneously.

Carving the body should be done first. There is a technique in doing this. First, you will want to draw out the shape of the top of the duck, similarly like you did with a figurine, but on a larger scale. You will want to use a compass to make a perfect circle in the diameter of the duck's neck. When preparing the block for the duck's head, you want to draw the same sized circle on the bottom of the smaller block. See Figure Fourteen below to see how the shapes should be drawn on the two blocks.

Figure Fourteen: The three pictures show how you should have the shapes of the ducks drawn

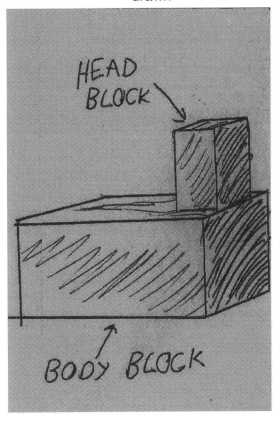
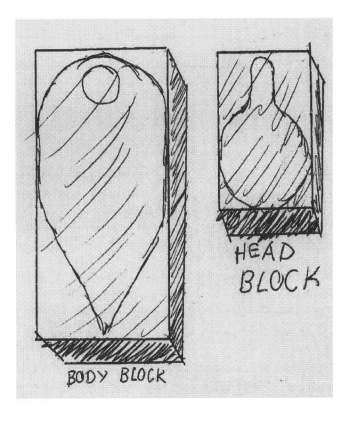

Figure 14a   Figure 14b

Notice that the two blocks shown in Figure 14a are well proportioned to each other. The duck's head is much smaller than the duck's body. This is why as Figure 14a illustrates, the block which the body is being carved out of is much bigger than the block the head is to be carved out from.

Figure 14b illustrates how you need to draw the lines and circles for the duck's body. You want to use a compass for drawing the circle. Circles have to be accurate because this forms the neck when the duck's head is glued to the body. The circles which form the diameter of the neck needs to be same size on the head block and on the body block.

Figure 14c illustrates how the circle for the upper part of the neck needs to be drawn on the bottom part of the block and the sides of the block should be the shape of the head and the beak. You also want to make sure that the circle on the bottom of the smaller head block is off to the rear end of the block to make room for the beak.

Carve the basic two dimensional shapes of the body and the head first. This has to be done in a special way as you want to carve the body with the top shape as the original two dimensional shape and the head, you want to carve the side as the two dimensional shape. See Figure Fifteen to see how the initial two dimensional shapes need to be carved.

Figure Fifteen: See the two images to see how you need to carve out the two dimensional

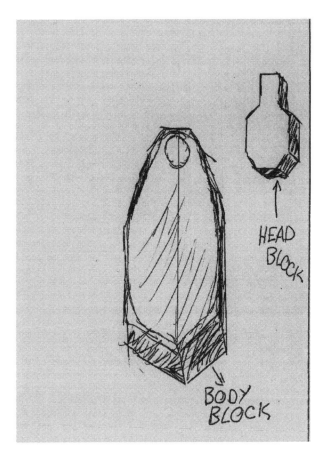

shapes of both the body and the head

Figure 15a   Figure 15b

Notice that in Figure 15a the body of the duck is being shaped from the sides of the block and the top and bottom are left alone. The head is the opposite, as illustrated in Figure 15b. In Figure 15b, you can see that the sides are left alone and the front and back are being carved out forming the initial shape of the duck's bill, head, and neck.

There is a reason for this. Basically, the circle drawn on the top part of the duck's body and the bottom of the duck's head need to fit together and have a seamless connection to make the neck look natural. You need to understand that the final product has to look like a real duck.

Carving out the finer details of the duck decoy is simply rounding off the edges of the body to shape the wings and carve around the neck area. You will want to carve the neck and keep it as conformed to the circumference of the neck as much as possible. See figure Sixteen below to see how the finished body should look like.

Figure Sixteen: The finished body of the duck decoy

Now, when you are roughly finished with the body, you will want to carve and shape the head. When you look at the duck in nature, you will see that the neck is thinner than the head. Start carving the top of the head first and then work your way to the bottom before carving the bill. When you are carving the neck, you want to make sure that it does not get thinner than the neck on the body. You need to remember that you can carve wood off the block, but you cannot put wood back on. When you remove wood, it's permanent. As the head gets shaped, you will want to place it on the body to see how close you are to the neck being the right size on both the body and the head as seen in Figure Seventeen below.

Figure Seventeen: Carving the head and seeing how it fits on the body.

Notice that above, in Figure 17, how well the head is carved and how it should fit perfectly to the body block. When gluing the head on, you should use a strong wood glue which you can sand to make smooth once it has dried and cured.

Tools needed for carving duck decoys are much the same tools as for figurines, but you won't need the carving needles as much as you would for figurines.

Gluing the head to the body is relatively easy. When you are sure that the neck connection on both the body and head are the same diameter, then use a good quality wood glue to glue them together. You can get high quality wood glues at any lumberyard or woodcarving shop.

Sanding your decoy is a necessity, as the surfaces have to be smooth. Glue the head to the body first, and make sure the glue you use is fully dried and cured before you sand. Sand first with a corse grit sandpaper and then with a fine grit sandpaper. Once the duck is fully sanded it's ready for painting.

Three dimensional woodcarving can be a very fulfilling art form and you can create many things from wood this way. Simply let your imagination take off, and you will see that you can create some amazing stuff.

Chapter Six

Using Woodcarving to Create your own Furniture

Not everyone could think in their wildest dreams that they can build their own furniture and create it to their own desire. It can be done and if your intent to learn woodcarving to make your own furniture, then you have come to the right place. In this chapter, you will learn the basics for making your own furniture and accents for your home by doing the following:

A. **Learning basic woodworking and cabinet making** to make your own kitchen cabinets, dressers, wardrobes, and other cabinets. You will learn how you can incorporate two dimensional woodcarving on the cabinet doors and sides, such as relief carving and chip carving.
B. **Making a headboard for your bed** on which you can carve your favorite patterns or images using relief and chip carving.
C. **Working with a lave** to make posts for your canopy or bunkbed. Once you know how to use a lave, you can also make the right balusters for banisters for stairs, railings for decks, porches, and balconies. You can also incorporate your three dimensional carving, such as your figurines as ornaments for some of your fancier furniture.
D. **Carving lattice using a jigsaw** from wood planks for decorative balconies, railings, fretting, and other fancy nooks and crannies needed to make unique furniture.
E. **Using a bandsaw** to make balusters from flat wooden planks with unique shapes.
F. **Using a drum sander** to make some unique edges for cabinet doors, dresser drawers, and more.

Learning Basic Woodworking and Cabinet Making

Before attempting to make your own furniture, you need to remember that woodcarving is only part of that. Up to now, you have learned the basics for both two and three dimensional woodcarving. Now it's time to take the skills you have just learned to the next level. Making your own furniture is a challenge and if done right, your interior will be the talk of the neighborhood.

Before you can make your own furniture, you will have to learn the basics of woodworking and cabinet making. This is important because it gives you the bare bones of what you are supposed to do when making your own furniture. There are many things which seem minor but can have a significant effect on how your pieces of furniture and cabinets can hold up to everyday use.

Making dovetails is key for making solid drawers for your dresser. What exactly are dovetails? Dovetails are the little wooden slots cut in the shape of a dovetail which are then glued together at a corner. This makes your drawer much stronger than if you were simply to nail the back of the drawer to the sides. You can cut the dovetails using your delicate saw, but there are also power tools with a special template which you can get for cutting dovetails. See Figure One below.

Figure One: Common dovetailing on the back of a drawer

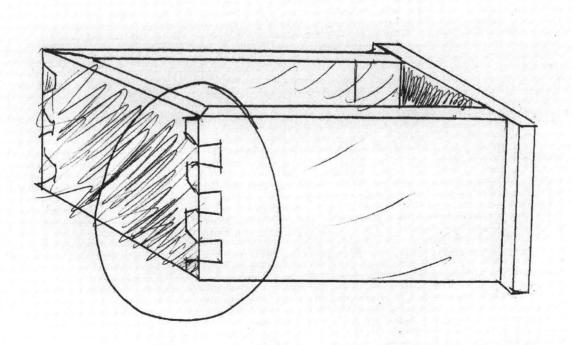

Notice that illustrated in Figure One, the dovetailing can also look very attractive when the drawers come out. Putting dovetails together is very simple. Simply use a strong wood glue to glue them together. The base of the drawer will make the drawer box stronger.

Making shelving can be used in both cabinet making and making bookcases for your library or study. Shelving can also be used in built in bookcases which can hold books, special souvenirs and keepsakes, collectibles, and more.

When making shelving, you can simply make a groove in the wood on the vertical sides of the shelves which you can then install special strips which you can get at any hardware store to adjust the shelves. These do look nice and you can also carve the edges of the shelves with chip carving for decoration.

The other way you can create shelving for a built in bookcase is more permanent and will not allow you to adjust the shelves. These permanent shelves can be designed to look very elegant with a facade trim which can be done with either chip or relief carving.

Making cabinet doors with beautiful carving on them is a great idea for wonderful home made furniture and kitchen cabinets. This can take a long time to do.   There are many different ways you can do this.

You want to first make your cabinet.   Make sure the doors fit properly and open and close properly before you begin carving. If you do the carving first, you will end up having to cut part of the cabinet doors and removing some of your work. This is why it is crucial to make the doors first. If you are not good at carpentry and cabinet making, then hire a carpenter or cabinet maker to make all the components for the cabinets. Then before hanging the doors and being sure everything fits all together, you can start carving the doors.

The easiest way to start, obviously is with chip carving. You can also do relief carving, but that can take longer.

The basics for carving the pattern you want to have on your cabinet doors need to fit the style of your home and your personal tastes. You need to know what your personal tastes are. We cannot choose that for you, however, we can advise you on how to get the ideas to co-inside with your personal tastes.

Basically, what are things which can reflect personal tastes. Basically, personal tastes can be influenced by your ethnic and cultural heritage, cultural interests, artistic tastes and interests, and more. The fact is your life and events in your life will influence your personal tastes and experiences. Sometimes, personal tastes can be influenced by places you have traveled to, homes you have visited, or even things you grew up with. The next step is to put your personal tastes on wood in either chip or relief carving.

Take a look at Figure Two below.   Notice that in Figure Two, back to the Georgian style minibar and grill. You can see that the chip carving on the cabinet doors of the minibar was actually influenced from a traditional Georgian woodcarving on the leg of a table from the 1700s.

Figure Two: The doors of the Georgian minibar

The artist who built this minibar was heavily influenced from numerous trips he made to the Republic of Georgia and bought different books about Georgian embroidery, woodcarving, and many other different art forms used in Georgian folk art.

Getting ideas for woodcarving on cabinet doors is very simple. You first need to come up with a theme and then get ideas which go with the theme. Themes can be broad and you can

use your creativity to create any theme you want.   Here are great sources for ideas for chip and relief carvings which you can use to get ideas. These are listed below.
  A. **Picture books with closeup photos** of different folk art patterns involving chip or relief carving. Picture books or coffee table books are a great idea for different folk patterns. We have gotten many of our ideas from different picture books. These are great ideas and you can sketch some of these patterns on paper then transfer it to the cabinet doors and begin carving.
  B. **Different how to books from foreign countries or states** are another great source of ideas. In our library, we have how to books for woodcarving, embroidery, landscaping, or other art forms from at least five different countries. If you can read and write in different languages, this can be an added benefit. We have discovered that many Russian books on how to do woodcarving for your home, you can see all kinds of popular woodcarvings which Russians use on their window decorations, doors, roof trim, and more. You can even take advantage of the designs shown in these books, even if you can't read the languages those books are published in. A picture can be a great idea getter and you can easily add onto that picture to create a design which is uniquely yours.
  C. **Carrying a personal sketch book or camera** to copy patterns you see on your travels. You can sketch designs you see, take photos (where allowed) and get all kinds of different ideas. Take note that some museums might not allow photos to be taken, thus if you are artistically inclined, you can easily get a sketchbook and sketch folk designs which you like.

Creating the look of antiquity can easily be done with your cabinet doors, some drawers, and other pieces of furniture can be done by using your U-gouger to gouge the corners of the wood to create the look of wear over time. A Dremel tool can also be used to create this effect. (See Chapter Eight)

Making a Headboard for your Bed
Another great way to display your woodcarving skills on your furniture is to create a fancy headboard for your bed. Headboards are the simplest pieces of furniture to create, as you do not have to build a trundle for your bed. In fact, a headboard is typically designed to be bolted to the head of a base trundle of a bed on which a mattress can be easily placed on. The basics of making a good headboard for your beds are as follows:

  A. **Purchase your bed trundle, spring box, and mattress first.** You want to know how high you want your headboard to be. To keep the headboard from falling, you will want to create some sort of support for the headboard which keeps it straight and parallel to the wall.
  B. **Decide the bed size before buying wood** for the headboard. You need to know the different bed sizes and dimensions before you can choose a headboard. These dimensions are covered below.
      1. **Single** is a bed which can only sleep one person. Typically this kind of bed is two and a half feet wide and six and a half feet long. The single bed can be designed to have a headboard at the head of the bed, which is common, but many designers will also have a single bed in a corner, so you can also create a headboard and side board for a fancy sleep cubicle.
      2. **Double bed** is a small two-person bed which can basically be the same size as two single beds put together.
      3. **Queen size bed** is a two-person bed which typically is six and a half feet long by six feet wide. This is a large bed typically designed for the master bedroom of a house and is very common for a married couple.

4. **King size bed** is typically the largest bed you can get. Typically a king size bed is seven feet long by six and a half feet wide. This bed offers ample room for tossing and turning.

C. **Decide on the shape of the headboard** and have it pre-cut by a professional if you do not have the right power tools to do it. Once you have the headboard pre-cut, you can take the necessary measurements and begin the next step.

D. **Draw the entire design** before you begin carving it. You always need to remember that when you carve off wood, you won't be able to replace it, so draw first, then carve. When drawing your design, you want to make sure the design covers a good portion of the headboard and geometric designs of chip carving are symmetrical and look evenly placed. This can be done by measuring where each design will be.

E. **Carve the design** and then you can finish it with a stain and varnish, as shown in the next chapter.

Fastening the headboard is typically done with large bolts which you can pick up at any hardware store. You will want to make sure you are able to fasten the headboard to the bed frame before you begin your carving.

Using a Lave
When making furniture or different nicknacks for your home, you will have to learn how to use a lave to make neat little details and almost all master woodcarvers know how to use a lave.

What is a lave? A lave is a special tool which is used to make decorative posts for beds, banisters, railings, frets, and other items for your home or furniture. The lave is partially a power tool in that it rotates a post and you hold one of the larger woodcarving knives to carve out round beads, balls, and other grooves from a square 4X4 post or larger.

The typical lave functions with a rotary vice which fastens one end of the wooden post to a wheel which turns freely and the other end of the post is also fastened to a rotary vice which is attached to a spinning apparatus connected to a motor. Once the post is fastened in place and you turn on the machine, the entire post will spin. Here is where you need to be careful. If not used properly, working a lave can be very dangerous.

Because the motor of a lave can spin the post at a very high speed, you need to be especially careful when beginning to carve out the post. You want to have a good grip on your knives or gougers when carving a post on a lave because if not held in a strong enough hold, the high speed of the lave can literally knock the knife or gouger out of your hand, potentially causing serious injury.

Typical knives used with a lave are the same as the large size carving knives which need a mallet for large chip carving. The different knives are listed below.

A. **The flat blade knife** is a little different from your standard woodcarving knife. This knife almost looks like a large wood chisel used in basic carpentry. This knife is typically used in making the post round. You simply hold the blade on the wood as it is spinning and it will cut off all the corners and eventually, you will eventually be able to have a round post. Use care in getting the carving started as the speed can hit the blade and you will feel the force in your hand. Find a comfortable position before you use this knife on a regular basis. Some laves will allow you to adjust the speed of the motor. This can make using the lave much safer, as you should use a slower speed when cutting the corners. You can then up the speed as the corners of the post have already been somewhat rounded.

B. **The 45 degree angle knife** at a much larger scale should also be used with caution. Main uses for the large 45 degree knife is to angle the cut from where the square part of the post is angled to the round part of the post.
C. **The U-gouger** can be used to make beads and grooves in the post and make it more fancy. You can use the U-gouger in several different ways to carve out beads and balls in your post.
D. **The V-gouger** can also be used to make sharp grooves in the post. Note that you can get special V and U-gougers made specifically for laves and they can be used with different sizes.

What can you use a lave for? Laves are one of the most advanced woodcarving tools. The lave can be used to make legs for tables and chairs, balusters for banisters and railings for balconies, lofts, and porches.

Working with a lave can be tricky at first, but once you have the hang of it, it can actually be quite fun. When mastering the lave, you will be amazed at what you can do with it. Looking at Figure Three below, you will see that the construction of the lave and the knives are quite simple.

Figure Three: The lave and all its components

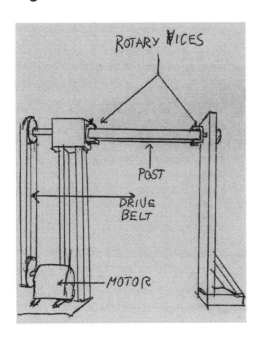

Figure 3a

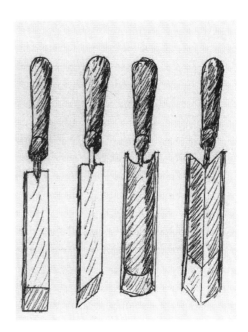

Figure 3b

In some cases, working with a lave can allow you to create some interesting posts for your home. For example, if you have a large enough lave, you are able to carve fancy pillars for a small front columns for the front door of your home. You can also make all the balusters for the banisters of your stairs, railings for lofts and balconies. The possibilities are endless.

Notice that the knives used with a lave look similar to large woodcarving knives which use a mallet. The only difference is that with these tools, you so not use a mallet. Also, one of these is square, like a carpenter's chisel. This knife is to make the post round. Laves come is different sizes for both large posts or for the round rods in more delicate work, such as fretting.

Using a lave for fretting inside your home is also a great idea, especially if you have bought an old Victorian home which needs renovation. Many old Victorian homes in the United States had fancy decorative fretting over their main doorways in the parlor and other main rooms of the home. Many of these frets have been destroyed or damaged over time as these homes have been left abandoned. The key to restoring fretting is to have a special lave which can carve small pieces of wood. Many decorative frets are made of pieces of wood which are ornately carved and can sometimes be made with a mixture of lave work and fancy latticing. Learning how to do lattice work will be mentioned below. Figure Four below is a perfect example of decorative fretting found in many old homes in the United States.

Figure Four: Decorative fretting over a major doorway in a Victorian home.

Notice that the rods in the fretting are rather small and the curve is also a mixture of latticing and small lave work. This is basically a modest diagram of a Victorian fretting over a doorway. Most fretting in Victorian homes are so complex and intricate that it is very difficult to put into a small image. The best way to get ideas for fretting is to go visit a Victorian home which has its original fretting inside. This can be hard to find, but it can be done.

Carving Lattice using a Jigsaw
Much woodcarving done for the home and furniture is done by carving lattice out of wood or planks using a jigsaw. Make it even more fancy when you use a jigsaw for the decorative holes in the lattice and woodcarving knives to add texture to the lattice and creating a fancy lattice work which can be great for moveable screens, decorative fretting for awnings or balconies and porches, and more. Latticing can also be made for enclosing unsightly sand and construction materials and other things under decks and porches.

Choosing the right wood for your lattice work is crucial. You want to avoid using plywood, especially for outdoor work. The problem with plywood is that most plywood is different wood particles which are glued together to make one sheet of plywood. There are different kinds of plywood on the market, including particle board, which is primarily used in home construction.

The biggest problem with plywood is that it can chip as you are carving it. If you are just jigsaw carving without gouging, then a high quality plywood can be used, however, it you plan to gouge and add texture, then you should find large planks of high quality wood, such as aspen, mahogany, walnut, and other high quality wood ideal for carving. Remember, however, hardwoods, like walnut, can be hard to carve. You want to remember that if you are just starting out in woodcarving. Planks are not large sheets, like plywood, but they can be quite wide and you can also fined wide boards of solid wood which are a series of planks glued together with an industrial grade glue that won't fall apart.

Planning and drawing out your lattice design should first be done on paper. You should always have a sketch of everything you make. This is like a plan to go by, like building a home, so to speak. You want to draw the areas where you want to cut out with a jigsaw and where you want to carve in standard chip carving. Once you are satisfied with the drawing, you want to transfer the design on the wood.

Carving on lattice work is usually done with chip carving, however, there are some lattices where relief carving and chip carving have been used simultaneously.

Using the jigsaw is imperative when carving out lattice work. What exactly is a jigsaw? A jigsaw is a special power saw which has a thin blade which osculates up and down at a very high speed and can carve organic shapes and holes in wood. Typically, when you think of jigsaws, you tend to think of jigsaw puzzles. These old wooden puzzles, where the pieces are cut in organic shapes which interlock with each other are cut with a jigsaw, hence the name *jigsaw puzzle*.

Typically, a jigsaw can be used by itself when you are cutting a shape from the side of the board, however, when you are using a jigsaw to cut out a hole of a particular shape, you will also need a drill with at least a half inch bit to drill a starter hole. Then you put the jigsaw blade in the starter hole and begin cutting out the shape by following the lines in the shape.

See Figure Five below to see what a jigsaw looks like. You can find a jigsaw at any Menard's, Lowe's, or Home Depot, or where ever else power tools are sold.

Figure Five: The typical jigsaw

Lattice work has commonly been used in a wide variety of different areas. Lattice work has been used in wooden iconostasis in Orthodox churches as screening between icons, Screens which are assembled with a series of hinged panels, decorative fretting under awnings and above balcony railings, and more.

Using a Band Saw

What is a band saw? Basically, a band saw is a saw which has a thin blade which spins like a band around two pulleys. Basically, the blade of a band saw is a thin flexible metal blade with fine teeth which can even be manipulated with your bare hands. The blade is a band which is tightly attached to two pulleys, one of which is driven by a motor and the band spins at a high speed and is designed to cut organic shapes in wood planks for fancy designs or organic shapes.

The band saw works much faster than a jigsaw and is primarily used for carving out shapes in the sides of planks for balusters for banisters, porch, and balcony railings. You can also use a combination of a band saw and a jigsaw for cuts in the center of the plank and on the side of the plank. Use the band saw for the sides of the plank and cut the sides of the planks first, then once all the sides of the planks are cut with the band saw, use the jigsaw to cut out the holes in the center and you can also use chip carving to add more character to your baluster planks.

Using a Drum Sander

What is a drum sander? A drum sander is a special sander which can do amazing things with wood. Unlike your typical sander which uses a flat sandpaper, a drum sander has special drums which can be affixed to the rotor drum of the sander. The drum sander is set up on a table with a guide fence and you are able to smooth edges of your work using a drum sander.

The sanding drums are basically like rolled up sand paper and you can get corse grit and fine grit sanding drums, just like you can get corse grit and fine grit sandpaper. The sanding drums spin at a high speed and with controlled manipulation, you can even use a drum sander to carve a special shape into the wood.

Uses of a drum sander can be amazing, as it can create that weathered effect to your dresser drawers and cabinet doors. You can also use your drum sander for carve and shape wood for making wooden toys, shaping wood trim to fit around natural stone, and more. Once you master using a drum sander, the possibilities of your creativity can be endless.

Basically, in this chapter, you learn to apply all the basic woodcarving techniques you have learned thus far and become more creative to make your own furniture, decorative nicknacks for your home and other things which can make your home and yard uniquely yours.

Chapter Seven

Stains, Varnishes, and other Finishes

Now that you have made your woodcarving masterpiece, you will want to know how you want to finish it. There are many ways to finish your work of art, ranging from painting, stains, and varnishes. You can also use oils to preserve your wood. In fact, when making wooden cutting boards, many people often cover them with olive oil to preserve the wood and prevent rot. Likewise, natural wood carvings, such as many chainsaw carvings (Covered in Chapter Nine) are often preserved with using old motor oil. Whatever finish you choose, you will learn how to do the following:

A. **Prepping your work** before finishing. You will learn how to sand parts or your work, cleaning all the work from dust and other particles which can ruin your finish.
B. **Choosing your stain** and how to manipulate the color of your wood using different stains.
C. **Proper application of stain** and the coating process of stain. The key to effective staining your wood to make the grains to show and enhance your work.
D. **Stain color and how to use it** is also key in choosing the appropriate stain for your work. Some stains are designed to enhance the color in different types of wood. Different woods have different colors and some stains can enhance that color, but if you use them with a combination of different colors on different woods, the results can be amazing.
E. **Varnishes** and how they are applied. There is a wide variety of varnishes on the market. Some of these varnishes have stains mixed with them and others are clear. Most varnishes are water soluble and while wet can be easily cleaned off of your brushes. You will also understand between the difference between polyurethane varnishes, resin varnishes, and how they should be applied.
F. **Painting** for those who do not desire the woodgrain look on their work. You will learn the difference between acrylic, latex, and alkyd paints. How they should be applied, and the different primers which are used for these paints.

How to apply primers and coats of paint when painting wood. Wood can be a temperamental surface to paint. If paint is not applied properly to wood, it can peal off and you can have serious issues with the actual wood, ranging from rot and other problems. This is important if you are choosing to paint your finished piece. This will be covered more below.

Prepping your Work
Before beginning to apply any finish to your woodcarving project, it is very important to learn how to properly prep your wood surface. Stains and varnishes are very temperamental and especially varnishes, are very sticky, so any kind of grain of dust or other particle can stick out like a sore thumb. Furthermore, if your surface is too corse, the varnish might not apply properly, causing an uneven coverage which can make your finish look too unprofessional and haphazard.

Before applying stains and varnish, you have to prepare the surface. Most good quality carving woods should already be pre-sanded and should already be smooth. If you are using raw wood for your carving, you should have already plained your wood before you begin your carving in the first place. Even with a plained wood, you should do some light sanding to make sure the surfaces are smooth. If you had to do some cutting, such as making cabinet doors or dresser drawers, you will have to sand those edges, as most saws will leave a corse surface after they cut the wood.

After sanding all the rough areas, you want to make sure that you place your work in a dust and impurity free environment. This is very important. Any grain of dust, any sawdust particle, any impurity can cause a blemish which you will later not be able to get rid of when you apply the stain, varnish or paint.

Why is dust so bad? Well, dust can interfere with the bonding. When it comes to stains, the dust can impair the application of the stain and keep it from soaking into the wood. This can cause the stain not to provide its full color potential into the wood. Varnish might not be able to bond well when there is poor bonding, you can have a problem with the varnish pealing. This also applies with paints and primers.

Choosing your Stain
What exactly is stain and how does it differ from paint? Both paints and stains give color to the wood. Paints, however, are opaque and mask the grain of the wood. Paints will also need a primer to help bond to the wood. This will be covered below in the paragraphs about proper paint application. Stains, on the other hand, also give color to the wood and also bring out the character of the wood.

Stains work as an oil based substance which can easily absorbed by the porous grains of the wood. You do not apply stains with a paint brush, like you would with paint or varnish. Typically, varnishes are actually applied properly with a dry rag. You want to make sure you do not apply too much stain as it could cause a stain spot.

Choosing stain color can be a bit tricky. Many hardware stores carry a wide array of different brands of stain and they all have their different lines of color which are usually aimed at enhancing the color of the most popular woods, such as oak, pine, walnut, cherry, and ebony. Creating a stain for ebony is kind of strange, as ebony is a rare wood and when found, it is very expensive. In fact, ebony can be even more expensive than teak.

Stains can also come with different colors and hues which can change the color of the wood and create non-natural colors, such as an orange tint, a blue tint, or even a pickle finish. The pickle finish is interesting in itself, as this gives the wood a white finish. Pickled stains are much harder to find, but it was a popular color in the 1970s. We will have a separate paragraph on pickling below, as this is a specific color which only works well on darker woods.

Different colors can also allow you to mimic different woods and create your own color by mixing your stains. When mixing, however, you don't mix stains by mixing them together like paints. When mixing stains, you add a different color in a separate coat and it will mingle with the other stains inside the wood. Different colors available at most hardware and home improvement stores, such as Menard's, Lowe's, or Home Depot are listed below. We tend to mention the names of the bigger store names, such as Menard's, Lowe's, and Home Depot because these are the stores where the vast majority of people shop at when they look for home improvement products. Some smaller home improvement stores and specialty shops might have even more options depending on the area where you live.

A. **Cherry red** is designed to enhance the reddish color of cherry wood. When applied to a white wood, such as aspen, basswood, or pine, this stain might have more of a purple color. Typically, it is a good idea to use this stain with other colors when staining.
B. **Honey oak** is a stain which is made primarily for white and red oak wood. This stain gives the oak wood a nice golden yellow honey color. This stain also works nicely on walnut, giving this already dark wood a darker golden brown look. Other woods which honey oak stain works on include aspen, basswood, pine, and mahogany.
C. **Burgundy wine** is a stain which is similar in color to cherry red. This stain is designed for darker woods with a reddish tone, such as cherry, red oak, mahogany, and can give these woods a beautiful deep red color. Using this stain by itself on white woods, such as aspen or basswood, it will give a Burgundy wine color. When using this with the above mentioned cherry red stain, you can turn a white wood into a dark reddish color giving a beautiful cherry look. Because stains bring out the grain of the wood and all the knots, you can use a white knotty pine and give the dark red look of a fine cherry look.
D. **Ebony** is a stain which is originally intended to enhance the already black color of ebony wood, but because ebony is such a rare and expensive wood to obtain, ebony stain can give a very nice charred look to your woods. When applied to white wood varieties, such as aspen, basswood, and pine, the ebony stain should be used simultaneously with another dark stain, such as walnut or cherry red. Use of ebony on white woods can make the wood look too grey, though if you like that look, you can always apply that. When ebony stain is used with red woods or dark brown woods, such as walnut, oak, cherry, you can have a darker charred look. Ebony does work very well with the unique greenish purple natural color of poplar.
E. **Walnut** gives a nice chocolate color to all the white woods. When you work with lighter woods, such as aspen, basswood, and pine, you might want to mix with a red stain, such as cherry red or burgundy wine color to add a more natural color of darker woods. Beginners will be using white woods, such as basswood or aspen, as these woods are softer and easier to carve.

When choosing your stain color, don't limit yourself with the colors mentioned above. You can look online and go to specialty stores do get more of the hard-to-get stains.

Proper application of stains is done simply by lightly dipping a cloth rag, such as an old T-shirt and rub an area and you want to rub the stain into the wood until you do not get any stain from the rag anymore. Then you repeat the process. Unlike paints, which cover the surface of the wood, stains will go into the wood. This is why you need to rub the stains into the wood.

Once you have rubbed all the areas in the wood with the stains, you will want to use a clean rag to wipe off all the residual stains and let the first coat soak into the wood. You want to wait overnight before you apply the second coat of stain.

Stain sampling should always be done before choosing to stain your work. Use a piece of scrap wood of the same type that your work is made from and choose from those sample colors before you stain your entire project.

Pickling your wood is a dying art form and requires a special type of stain. This can look interesting with some chip and relief carvings. When you pickle your wood, you give your wood a white milky color and this works nicely with darker woods, such as walnut, poplar, cherry, and oak. Very popular in the 1970s, pickling was used as a method of staining paneling, furniture, and other works made from wood. This today is known as either *kitsch* or *cliche*. Basically, pickling is a white milky stain which is often mixed with varnishes and does involve a complicated process.

Prepping your stained surface for varnishing is a must for your varnish to stick to the work and look professional. Basically, you do not want to varnish your project for at least three days to a week before you apply the varnish. Stains are primarily oil based and must be fully dried before you can even attempt to apply a varnish or other type of similar finish. It will take a stained wood much longer to dry than wood sprayed with some kind of water based solution. Oils take a lot longer to dry, thus you want to make sure that your project is dry to the touch before you apply the varnish.

Do not use any heat drying or hot air dryers to dry stained woods. You need to remember that stains are highly flammable because they are oil based.

Varnishes
A varnish is typically a clear finish which can be applied directly to the wood without any kind of primer. There are different types of varnishes, some of which are water soluble and some of which are oil based. Some varnishes are mixed with a stain, but we don't recommend those types of varnishes. You're much better off staining first, then varnishing.

Properly applying varnish is crucial if you want your finish to last. The first thing you need to know before applying your varnish is what types of varnishes there are and which ones are the best for the right situation. Any urethane is a good varnish. These are water soluble and is easy to clean. Furthermore, they are hard coats and give a nice look to your project and can handle almost anything life throws at it. Some of the common varnishes are listed below.

A. **Spar Urethane varnish** is a good outdoor varnish. Spar urethane varnish is also considered marine varnish and is often used on wooden boats or on the wooden decking on ships. The average life of a spar urethane varnish can be 20 years or more. This varnish can come in either a glossy, satin, or matte finish. We always like the glossy finish as it gives a nice shine to the wood and brings out all the grains together with the color of the stains in the wood. Satin and matte finishes do not have a high gloss when dry.
B. **Polyurethane varnish** is often used for making the finish of hardwood floors and gym floors. This is also a good varnish for furniture as it is a durable finish and is highly scratch resistant. Polyurethane varnishes typically come in high gloss and satin finishes.
C. **Shellack** is a varnish primarily for artistic woodcarvings and wood crafts which do not endure high foot or hand traffic. This is great for your relief carving pictures, chip carved boxes, etc.

Resins

Resins are different from varnishes. Though they are liquid and are applied much the same way as varnishes, they are different. Resins have more the properties of glues and are very sticky. This is the reason why when working with resins as a finish for your project, you do not want to use paint brushes, which you can get away with when varnishing. When applying resins to your project, you want to use special foam rubber brushes which you can find in the paint department of any home improvement store. Resins have a harder coat than varnish and can last much longer than many varnishes. We recommend using resins if your woodcarving project is in a high moisture area.

Treating your Project with Oils

Oils are a great way to finish your woodcarving project. Though oils won't enhance the wood's color like stains do, it does act as a great preservative for wood in high exposure areas.

As a rule of thumb, any oil will preserve wood. Whether you use olive oil, vegetable oil, or a petroleum based oil, such as motor, it will preserve your wood. The reason why oils will preserve wood is because wood is by nature porous.

Wooden cutting boards need to be treated with either olive oil or another type of vegetable oil before they can be used in the kitchen. You may have wanted to carve out a wooden cutting board or wooden bowls, you need to use the oil treatment and not varnish if you want to use them with food. The reason for this is that varnishes and any other petroleum based product can be toxic and should not be in areas where food is prepared. Virgin olive oil is ideal when treating your wooden cutting boards and bowls. The reason is because virgin olive oil is pure and will not affect the flavor of any food which comes into contact with the treated surface.

Chainsaw carvings and natural wood carvings can be treated with motor oil if you want to keep their natural look. Motor oil will possibly blacken the wood, but that can wear away. Motor oil will keep your projects from rotting and make them last a good 20 to 30 years. Do keep note, that despite the fact the oils preserve the wood, you will have to retreat your work periodically to keep them from cracking and coming apart.

Linseed oil can also be used in treating wood which is outside. In fact, linseed oil is often used in treating deck planking. The nice thing about linseed oil is that it will help with keeping the sunlight from causing wood from curing up and cracking. Use linseed oil for your fences and gates around your yard.

Paints and Primers

Many of you who like to carve figurines might prefer painting, especially since most figurines are designed to mimic real people and animals. Sometimes paints can work better for this genre of woodcarving than stains, varnishes, and oils. One thing you need to know, however, before you start painting your wooden figurines or other wooden projects is that painting on a wooden surface can be difficult and you may need to have a primer before you paint. There are many different paints with different bases out there and all of them require different primers. Some modeling paints may not even require primers as they may be made to bond directly to the wood.

Different types of paints which are commonly used on wood and wooden figurines and sculptures. These paints are different and some may be used in other countries versus others. A list of common paints are listed below.

A. **Acrylic** is a common base for many paints. Acrylic paints are often used in modeling paints which can be used on wood surfaces also. Though some acrylic paints might not require primers, you may want to read the instructions before you apply the paints. Acrylic is a synthetic substance which can sometimes mimic oil based paints.
B. **Oil** is a base for paints too, but this is not as common anymore as it was in the past. Most oil based paints do require a primer on wood.
C. **Alkyd** is an oil based paint which is not used as much in the US anymore, but is still used in Europe and the former Soviet Union. Alkyd does have some lead in it, thus care needs to be used when working with alkyd paints. Alkyd paints do need a primer for wood. Use alkyd paints in a well ventilated area.
D. **Latex** are the most common paints used in the United States. Latex is basically a rubber polymer and latex paints are water soluble. Latex does require a primer when applied to wood.

Primers basically work as a bonding agent. Typically, a primer works by bonding to the wood and filling in the pores made from the natural grains of the wood. Typically, you may want to have two coats of primer before you apply your paint.

Different paints require different primers. You want to check what type of the above mentioned bases your paint is before choosing the right primer. Choosing the right primer is crucial, because the primer has to match the base of the paint you are using. For example, you cannot use an acrylic based primer for oil or alkyd based paint. Likewise, You cannot use a latex primer for oil based paints. The base of the primer must match the base of the paints you are using.

Primer colors are mute. Basically, the primer does not have a color so to speak. The main function of the primer is to act as a bonding agent and not to give color. Most colors of primers can range from off white to grey, yellow, or pink. It is deliberate that primers have an off color. This is so it will not affect the colors of the paints that are painted over the primers.

The composition of paint is rather simple. Typically, paints have a bonding base, be it acrylic, oil, alkyd, or latex. The colors come from different pigments. There are different kinds of pigments and it's the pigments which give the paint its color. In many cases, pigments used in paints can be mineral and metal oxides or other natural or artificial substances.

Paints for figurines can be found at any hobby shop or big hobby stores, such as Joann Fabrics, Hobby Lobby, or Michaels. Many small hobby shops can also carry a different variety of paints for figurines. If you shop at the bigger stores, however, you may need to pay attention. For example, going into the big stores, like Hobby Lobby, Michaels, or Joann Fabrics do carry a wide variety of acrylic based paints for all kinds of different arts and crafts. It is unclear whether these paints need a primer for wood or not. You want to double check by looking up the paint's manufacturer online. The manufacturer's website should be able to tell you whether a particular paint requires a primer or not. In some cases, if a primer is needed and cannot be found in the stores, you should be able to order it from the manufacturer.

Painting furniture and carved house details can be done the same way as you would figurines, but on a larger scale. Depending on the kind of furniture and what house details you are looking to paint, you may want to go to a home improvement store, such as Lowe's,

Menard's, or Home Depot and find a person in the paints department to help you find the right paints and primers.

Outdoor wooden features must be painted with a weatherproof paint. There are many latex paints available for this.

Mixing paints can be done to get your own specific color. Many stores will do that, however, if you want less limits, you may want to go to a specialty paint shop, such as Sherman Williams, which is not only a store but a whole brand of paints as well. There, they can guide you what colors will work well together and offer the right primers as well.

When painting your project, you will also have to know how many coats of paint are needed. As a rule of thumb, most paints require at least three coats before completion of the paint job. We recommend at least one or two coats more than that to allow the paints to fully give color to your project.

Chapter Eight

Enhance your Woodcarving with the Dremel Tool and other Power Tools

Up to now, you have learned to do woodcarving mainly with manual tools, such as the different knives and gougers, and a limited number of power tools, such as jigsaws and band saws. Here you will learn more about power tools and what you can do with them. In this chapter, you will learn the following:

A. **Using the Dremel tool** and what the Dremel tool is. You will see how compact the Dremel tool is and the wide array of bits which are available for the Dremel tool.
B. **Tricks with the jigsaw** which you have not learned in Chapter Six. Since you already know about the basics of a jigsaw, you can actually learn all the other things you can do with a jigsaw. Learn how to make jigsaw puzzles, cutting boards, and more.
C. **Carving with a drum sander** is another type of woodcarving which can open a whole new world for you. Using a drum sander, you can do all kinds of neat things. You will learn how to make wooden cars, animals, such as fish, and more. Using the drum sander and the Dremel tool together can allow you to make all kinds of interesting toys for your children and grandchildren.
D. **Carving fence and deck posts with a skill saw** for your outdoor projects. This is a neat little project. You can actually use your skill saw to add detail and spires to your fence posts for a wooden picket fence or for added beauty to your deck around your home.
E. **Using a router** to make signs, address markers, and many other things where you can quickly carve lettering into wood. Routers also come with templates for letters which you can put together for even spacing and allow you to make almost anything.

Working with a Dremel Tool
The Dremel tool is an amazing little compact power tool which can do almost anything. Not only is it great for woodcarving projects, but you can even use it on metal and other surfaces, provided you have the right bits for it.

What exactly is a Dremel tool? The Dremel tool has been a compact power tool which has been manufactured in the United States since 1932 and it is designed to do and reach in such small areas where typical power tools would not be able to reach. Dremel began manufacturing its Dremel tool in the 1930s when power tools were just becoming popular as many American households already had a reliable source of electricity.

Back then, when the Dremel tool was first manufactured, most power tools were rather large and cumbersome. In fact, many people would make their own power saws and drills with a simple motor which was attached to a pulley that could spin a belt, turning a circular saw blade or other type of woodworking device.

The Dremel tool was revolutionary simply because it is compact and can easily be manipulated with one hand to work in tight places where manual work would have taken a long time and be very tedious.

How can the Dremel tool help my woodcarving projects? Well, basically, the Dremel tool has a wide variety of different bits which range from small drum sanders to router bits and other engraving bits for making fine lines and other markings in the wood.   See Figures One and Two below to see what is in your typical Dremel tool kit.

Figure One: The Dremel tool inside its kit box with all the bits together

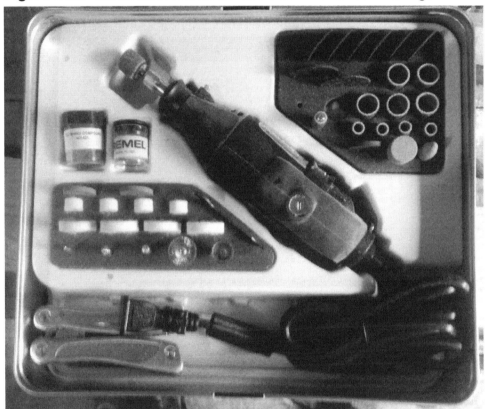

Notice in the above image, the Dremel tool has a small drum sander bit on its tip. These small sanding bits can be very handy when it comes to shaving or plaining sides of doors to make

then open and close properly. In some cases, the Dremel sanding bit, as seen on the Dremel tool in this photo can also give an old fashioned plained look to your sides of doors, drawers, or other crafts which can be created in half the time it would take a hand plain to do.

Notice that in the kit, in which the Dremel tool comes with, you can see a wide variety of different sanding drums and fine tuning bits. These are shown in more detail in Figure Two below.

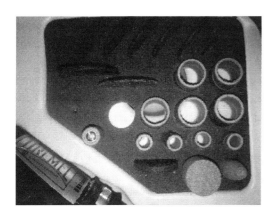 

Figure Two: The different components of the Dremel tool kit
          Figure 2a   Figure 2b

As seen above in Figure Two, the basic Dremel tool kit comes with a nice array of sanding bits and buffing bits as well. Keep in mind that not all the bits shown in this kit are for woodcarving or woodworking. Others can be used for woodworking and other work as well.

Figure 2a shows a series of small drum sanding bits which, as mentioned above, can be used for sanding small areas on your projects where other power tools cannot get into. Also, if you notice at the bottom right hand corner of Figure 2a, some of the sanding bits have different shapes. One of the sanding bits has an elliptical or torpedo like shape. This bit is great for getting into small tight areas, such as holes you would like to smooth out, like eyes, nostrils, or parts of a mouth if you were carving a large wooden sculpture of an animal or person.

Figure 2b shows some of the other bits which come in the basic Dremel tool kit. Most of the bits shown in Figure 2b are mainly for metal working, such as the soft white buffing bits and the wire brush bits, but the bits shown at the bottom left hand corner of Figure 2b are router bits which can be used on wood.

When it comes to using the Dremel tool, don't limit yourself to just the items which come in the basic Dremel tool kit. You can go to almost any woodworking specialty shop which sells power tools and find the Dremel tool there. It is a popular tool which both hobbyists and professional contractors buy, so Dremel tools are readily available.

There are many accessories which are made for the Dremel tool. If you go to the **www.dremel.com** website, which is the official website of the Dremel tool, you can see all the accessories they have available for this wonderful tool. You also need to watch for imitations when looking to purchase the Dremel tool. There are many brands which call themselves a name similar to the Dremel tool, but Dremel is a brand which has been on the market for a long time and the imitations do not match up to it. When you go to their website, the accessories for their rotary tools, which is the basic Dremel tool which Dremel is famous for, the bits and accessories are phenomenal and they have something for everything. In the paragraphs below, you will see all the bits you can get for the Dremel tool which you will need for your woodcarving projects.

Routing bits are needed if you are looking for something to engrave lettering in your woodwork. Though you could carve lettering by hand, it is very tedious and with a routing bit on your Dremel tool and a template, you can have even lettering which looks professional. Routing is ideal for making signs for your address and family name at home, a sign with the name of your business, or signs depicting your sense of humor. The possibilities are endless.

When it comes to routing, you can do some routing with a Dremel tool, but in some cases, getting a larger router might be a better choice for routing lettering. Routers will be covered below. The Dremel tool, however, can do a good job routing smaller pieces where lettering does not take up the entire project.

The Dremel tool does come with about ten different routing bits which you can use to have different angled grooves. You can also get a six piece bit kit for your Dremel tool which has basically every type of groove you will need.

What to and what not to rout with your Dremel tool can be a bit complicated. Typically, unless the lettering is small, you should not attempt to do any major lettering with the routing bits available for your Dremel tool. However, if you want to carve a straight groove into a sign or round an edge and add a bead to your work, the Dremel tool can be a great device to do that with.

Carving and engraving is where the Dremel tool is good at. You have a wide variety of carving and engraving bits available for your Dremel tool which you can use to do some very fine work on your woodcarving projects. Some of the carving and engraving bits which you can get for your Dremel tool have a fine bit on them where you can finish out some of the finest details on a work whether it is two or three dimensional woodcarving.

Cutting and shaping can also be done with a Dremel tool. There are circular blades among the Dremel rotary accessories available which can be used on wood and other surfaces as well. These circular blades are small and can be used to cut off undesired parts off of a work without damaging it.

Accessory kits can also be the best way to go when it comes to buying accessories for your Dremel tool. If you are planning to get an accessory kit for your Dremel tool, the mega kits can be the best way to go. The reason is that most of Dremel's mega kits can have up to 708 pieces or more. Though these mega kits may have bits for wood and other projects too, they can have all the routing bits, engraving and carving bits, rotary blades, and other special accessories for your woodcarving projects in them. Furthermore, as an added bonus, the mega kits can also contain pits for other projects around the house which you never know you might need someday.

When it comes to the Dremel tool, many avid woodcarvers have one and use it for certain applications. Though most of your woodcarving should be done manually with special woodcarving tools mentioned in the previous chapters of this book, the Dremel tool can be a nice addition as some works may require some detail carving which can be done with an accurate compact power tool like the Dremel tool.

Tricks with the Jigsaw
You may have learned how to use a jigsaw in Chapter Six about using your woodcarving skills in making your own unique furniture. The jigsaw, however, can be used in a wide array of neat nicknacks in woodcarving. You can use a jigsaw for doing all kinds of woodcarving projects ranging from window, roof, and trim details, wooden jigsaw puzzles, organic shaped cutting boards, and more.

How does a jigsaw work? Basically, if you remember from Chapter Six, a jigsaw is a power saw which as a thin osculating blade which moves up and down at a very high speed. Do not get a jigsaw confused with its larger counterpart, the Sawzall. The Sawzall is a large high powered saw which looks like an oversized jigsaw, but it is used by carpenters for cutting timbers when cutting a hole in a wall or in the floor for a staircase or something else which is major remodeling. You do not need such a powerful saw for woodcarving.

The jigsaw is a saw which stands upright and has a flat guide which goes around the blade. This guide helps guide the jigsaw blade and keeps it straight. Keeping a jigsaw blade straight is important because it is thin and can snap very easily.

Working with a jigsaw can be a bit difficult at first, but once you get the hang of it, you will find that in some of your woodcarving projects, the jigsaw can actually become your best friend. The most critical part of using the jigsaw is getting the cut started. Making sure that the blade is right on the line and does not veer from the line and cut off what it's not supposed to. This can be a big challenge, especially for smaller finer detailed parts of your work. Learning how to use your jigsaw for all kinds of woodcarving projects are just below in the next few paragraphs.

Carving a jigsaw puzzle is one of the most popular and common uses of the jigsaw. In fact jigsaw puzzles are called exactly that because in the old days, when the pieces were large and made from wood, a jigsaw was actually used to cut the pieces out.

Cut large pieces when you are planning to make a jigsaw puzzle for your children or grandchildren. Jigsaws are not made to cut very small tight curves like the Dremel tool is capable of.

When cutting a jigsaw puzzle, you want to cut the pieces first, sand them to get rid of any corse edges, and then put them together like a blank canvas. Once you have cut and sanded all the pieces for your jigsaw puzzle, you can put them together to make sure all the pieces fit together, and then you can get creative. If you are very artistic and like to paint, you can then paint the individual pieces of the jigsaw puzzle and make a picture which can be put together.

You can also carve some kind of basic image and then cut the pieces using your jigsaw, however, there is a caveat when you do this. Jigsaws like smooth surfaces, so don't attempt to make a jigsaw puzzle with any chip or relief carved images. Also, even if you did a chip or relief carved image for your jigsaw puzzle and cut bottom up, the blade of the jigsaw can cause some of the image or pattern to chip off and that can also ruin your work.

Another great idea for your jigsaw puzzle is to laminate a photo onto all the pieces. This can easily be done by having a favorite photograph blown up to the size of your jigsaw puzzle area. You can then trace the individual pieces onto the photo and cut them with an X-acto knife and laminate them onto the individual pieces of the puzzle.

Roof and trim details is an art form which uses a jigsaw and is highly popular in eastern Europe and parts of Asia. Cultures which are known to ornately carve window shutters, roof trim, balusters for railings and banisters include Russia, Lithuania, the Carpathian people of western Ukraine, Poland, Georgia, Germany, China, and Japan to name a few.

Doing a roof detail is complicated and you do need a jigsaw to do that. Typically, depending on what culture you are interested in doing and like, there is a large array of resources available to you on the internet and public libraries about different wood carved details for roofs and roofing trim. When learning how to do a roof detail, in this book, we will show you how to make a horse pattern for the pinnacle of a roof's gable, common on many rural Lithuanian homes. You can see on Figure Three below, the type of roof detail we are looking to make.

Figure Three: The roof detail of a Lithuanian home

Notice that in the above Figure Three, the wooden trim on the pinnacle of the gable are of two horses in a galloping fashion with the backs against each other, forming an X shape at the top of the gable. This photo was taken from the roof of the garage of a home of Lithuanian immigrants in Michiana, Michigan.

Making this type of trim detail can be a bit tricky because if you cut one board completely through, you could have one side which is weaker and with freezing temperatures causing melting snow to refreeze into ice, the expanding of the freezing water can cause the weaker part of the gable accent to come off. For this reason, you want to have a strong enough jigsaw which can cut through a 2X12 board. When doing anything involving the roof of your home, you don't want to use anything thinner than 2. They do make heavier duty jigsaws for this. Jigsaws come in a variety of different sizes and have different blade lengths.

In Figure Four below, you can see what you need to do to keep from cutting completely through one of the trim boards. You want to cut an even cut on both boards using a skill saw about half way into the board. Then you can carve out the middle using a wood chisel to have a notch in both boards where they are to cross. Once you see the notch is correct and the two boards fit how you want them to, then you can go on with the carving.

Figure Four: The notch for the crossing of the two boards

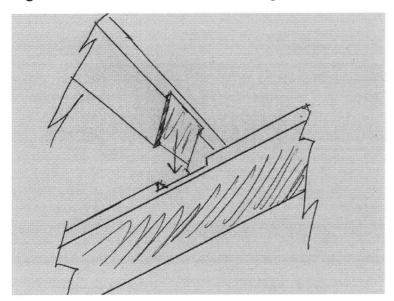

Once the basic woodworking is done so it is structurally sound, you can start by carving the shape of the horses using your jigsaw. This is done by first drawing out the shape of the horses on the boards, as seen in Figure Five below.

Figure Five: Drawing the shape of the horses on the boards

Keep in mind that when you do this, you want to take all measurements that the carved details will not interfere with the structural positioning of the boards, as they need to be set so you can place the drip edge for the roofing material on your home. These measurements need to be done before you cut the notches in and everything has to fit in the right place.

Once you have drawn the shapes and are ready to cut, carefully begin cutting with your jigsaw. You may have some space before you actually cut along the lines which draw out the shape of the horses. When this is the case, you want to cut at an angle so you can cut right along the lines.

While cutting, you want to watch the blade. Most jigs on the jigsaw have an arrow which shows the actual positioning of the blade. Make sure that arrow is on the line. If it is on the line, then the blade will be cutting right on the line. Once you have the horses cut, you can do any chip or relief carving on the horses to make them look more interesting and install them on the roof.

Cutting overhangs from the edge of the eves of the roof follows much of the same techniques as mentioned above when cutting the details for the pinnacle of your gables. Simply follow the design which you choose and then use the jigsaw to do the cutting.

Intricate pieces of woodcarving can also require the work of a jigsaw. In Chapter Six, you learned how to carve lattice work using a jigsaw, but here, you will learn what more you can do when making intricate woodcarvings involving holes inside your woodcarving.

Some chip and relief carvings which involve images of animals and people can be very intricate and may have holes in the work to either place a different colored wood or cloth behind to make it stand out.

To start, as mentioned in Chapter Six, you want to avoid using plywoods when using broad boards for carving large screens or other types of lattices or other dividers. You can find fine wood boards which are glued together made from some of the finest carving woods. Many places, like Menard's do sell these already plained and sanded. They are even wrapped in plastic for extra protection during transport.

When using your jigsaw to cut holes inside the board, you will want to use a drill to bore a hole in the area where you want to cut. If your hole has a sharp point, that is the best place to drill the starter hole. Then you can run the jigsaw around the organic lines of the hole until it's completely cut out.

Like the Dremel tool, the jigsaw is also a very versatile tool which can help you carve larger works for either furniture or other projects for your home or family.

Carving with a Drum Sander
Drum sanders are a great tool for woodcarving and woodworking in general. What exactly is a drum sander and how does it differ from a regular flat or belt sander? Well, basically, a drum sander has a drum on which a sanding drum is tightly fitted on. There are different types of drum sanders on the market and they are sold at large home improvement stores, like Menard's, Lowe's, and Home Depot.

Many drum sanders have a sticky rubber bit on which you fit the sanding drum on. You want to make sure that the drum is made for the sanding bit of the drum sander you buy. This is very important because the sanding drum has to be very tight on the bit so it won't move and spin on the sander as you are sanding wood on it.

Things you can do with a drum sander are limitless. You will learn some of the main things you can do with a drum sander in this chapter. In Chapter Six, you learned a little bit about using a drum sander when making furniture, but here, you can learn anything from making toys, such as wooden cars to animals for your children and grandchildren to shaping wood into organic shapes in a different format than you would be able to do with a jigsaw.

Making toys is a fun project using a drum sander. If you have children or grandchildren, this can be a fun project which you can include them in with. Though a child should not use any power tool without supervision, a drum sander is the least dangerous tool for them to use with your supervision as it does not have any blades which can cut like power saws and the Dremel tool can have. The only safety concern with a drum sander is that fingers should not touch the sanding drum as it is spinning, because it will sand off the skin and muscle.

Carving out a toy car can be one of the easiest things to do with a drum sander. To carve a car out of a wood block using a drum sander, all you need to is to draw the shape of the car on one side of the block and then simply let the drum sander do the work. You need both corse and fine grit sanding drums which you can use for all the course of the carving.

Use the corse grit sanding drums to begin the sanding of the wood block. You will be amazed at how fast the drum sander can dig into the wood. As a matter of fact, when sanding, you don't want to have the piece of wood in one place too long, as it will dig deep into the wood before you know it.

When shaping the wood block into a car, start sanding with the corners and gradually follow the sanding motion along the shape of the line drawn on the block. You may have to stop every once in a while, as drum sanders tend to produce a lot of saw dust and this needs to occasionally be cleaned off so you don't loose site of the line you drew on the wood block.

As you get the shape carved out according to the lines you drew on the block, then you will want to change the sanding drum from the corse grit to the fine grit. Use the fine grit sanding drum to fine tune the shape of the car. You can also use the fine grit sanding drum to round off the edges and make the car look as real as possible.

When finished sanding the car into shape, you need a drill to bore holes for the wheel axels to be placed. Many woodworking shops will sell wooden wheels for wooden toy cars. You can get a whole kit with the wheels and the axels and have them ready. One caveat with the wheels, however, is about painting. If you want to paint your wooden car, you should paint it before you put the wheels on so no paint can get on the wheels.

If making toy cars become a hobby of yours, a good idea for getting materials to do this is to visit a Boy Scouts supply store. The Cub Scouts and Webelos division of the Boy Scouts of America have a race for the kids called the *Pinewood Derby.* If you were in the Cub Scouts or Webelos, you probably remember the Pinewood Derby. The Boy Scouts do sell kits for making the Pinewood Derby cars. These kits come with a wood block made from white pine, a set of four wheels with the axels, and instructions.

Simply apply all the instructions above from the pine block in the Pinewood Derby car kit. This can be a great project if your children are involved with the Boy Scouts, either as a Boy Scout as a den chief for the Cub Scout troop or as a Cub Scout or Webelos.

Carving animals out of wood using the drum sander is another fun project you can do together with your children or grandchildren. Carving animals out of wood using a drum sander is much the same as making a car, but without the wheels. The one thing with carving out animals is that you might want to use the drum sander for all the major shaping, but some animals may have small nooks and crannies which the drum sander might not get into, thus you might want to use the Dremel tool to do the finer details.

Carving Fence and Deck Posts with a Skill Saw

Another simple woodcarving technique you can do using simple power tools is using a skill saw to carve fancy ridges into fence or deck posts. Add some chip carved ornamentation on the posts, and you will have something which can be the talk of the block. This can be very easy to do if you know how to properly use a skill saw.

Though many of the large home improvement chains, such as Menard's, Lowe's, and Home Depot carry pre-assembled fencing for picket fences, you can also make your own fence pickets, though that could cause the project to take longer. The fencing, however, is not what we're interested in here. We are more interested in the posts for your fencing or decking.

Upon working with your skill saw, you will notice that you can adjust the angle of the blade and how it cuts the wood. Though a skill saw is not a miter saw, it can cut at a 45 degree angle, and that's all you need.

Cutting a notch around all four sides of your fence post is the easiest to do. All you need to do is set the blade on your skill saw to a 45 degree angle and cut across the post from one end to the other. We recommend you use something as thick as a 4X4 or a 6X6 for a fence or deck post when you do this. Those posts are thick enough that the skill saw will not be able to cut through it. Do the same thing on the other side and repeat this process on all the other sides of the post. See Figure Six below on cutting the notch around the entire post.

Figure Six: The beginning of the notch cut into the post.

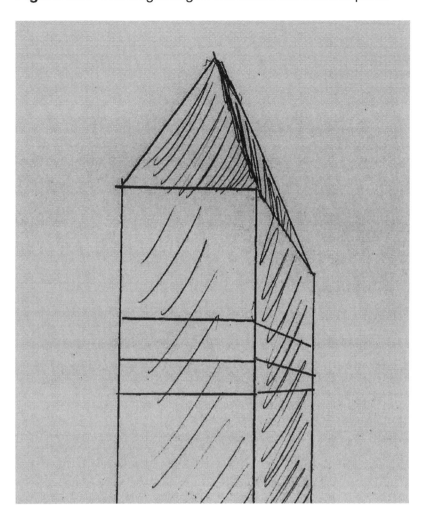

Typically, you can cut the pyramid top of the fencepost by setting your skill saw blade to a 45 degree angle and make sure the rotor blade of the saw is set to go as deep as possible. You then cut all four sides.

Making the pyramid point on the top of your fence post can be a bit more challenging. A skill saw might not be able to cut this deep. When doing this, you might want to use a miter saw and adjust the blade at a 45 degree angle. Most skill saws do have a miter template by the blade which you can adjust. See Figure Six below to see how this is done.

Figure Seven: The four images below show how to cut the pyramid point on your fence post

Whether you do this for your front picket fence or for your deck posts, having a fancily carved post at each segment can make your property unique from the neighbors. If you add chip carving, such as circles made from a series of carved out triangles, then you have a real fancy setup which can be the talk of the town.

Using your skill saw to carve notches into posts doesn't even have to stop with fence or deck posts. Want to build a pergola or fancy portal, you can use the same techniques and incorporate what you learned above with using a jigsaw for a spectacular effect on your home and yard.

Using a Router
A router is a unique power tool which can be used in all kinds of woodcarving projects for inside and out. A router is basically a tool which uses a high speed cutting bit to carve grooves into the wood. You can actually use these grooves to make lines and borders for signs and you can even carve letters into wood using a router. In fact, using a router to carve letters in wood for a sign of some sort is a popular thing to do.

The type of router bit you use can determine what type of groove you can carve in your wood. Some router bits are not designed for lettering, but for making a bead along the edge of your wood. This can be used simultaneously with carving letters into a wooden sign for your home or business.

When using a router bit, you will notice each bit has a different shape and can do a different kind of a groove into the wood. When carving in lettering, you may want a router bit which will have a flat groove, especially if the lettering you are carving into the wood is rather large. Some router bits can also make the depth of the groove you are carving into the wood as either being a V shape or a U shape.

Carving lettering can be very difficult and unless you have experience in using a router on a professional setting, you do not want to carve lettering without using a specific template. Any home improvement store which sells routers should also be able to sell templates of different letters and styles. Templates are typically made from a special metal which the router blade cannot cut through. You can use the templates as a guide for your router and it will cut within the template.

If you are a power tool guy, then this chapter should have all the information you need to know. We do not recommend that you limit yourself only to power tools, however. Power tools are nice for lots of difficult cutting, but there are some things which are just meant to be carved by hand. Some intricate carvings, such as chip and relief carving are so ornate that even a fine detailed power tool, like the Dremel tool would not be able to work.

Chapter Nine

Chainsaw Carving

For those of you who have a bit of the lumberjack inside of you, then this chapter is for you. One of the growing new trends in woodcarving is chainsaw carving or tree trunk carving. This is basically woodcarving on a large scale. This is a fun, but can also be a dangerous hobby. In this chapter you will learn the following:

A. **Chainsaw safety** is the first thing you need to know before you get into this kind of woodcarving. You can do amazing things with a chainsaw, but you need to remember that the chainsaw will spin on a bar at a very high speed, thus there is some force involved when working with a chainsaw.
B. **Other tools needed with the chainsaw** when embarking on chainsaw carving. You can incorporate using other power tools, such as the Dremel tool, power drills, and sanders.
C. **The history of chainsaw carving** and how the art evolved. You will learn about the Pacific Northwest Indians and their totem poles, which is the influence of most of the chainsaw carvings you see today. You will learn how chainsaw carving, then called log carving was originally done with axes and hatchets to do the work of the chainsaw today. You will see that chainsaw carving is not a new art form, it was done before with manual tools and took twice as long.
D. **Examples of chainsaw carving** which have been placed in other people's yard will be shown in this segment. You will be able to learn how you can do this with friends or by yourself.
E. **Working with natural wood** and what can be expected when you carve from a natural tree trunk. You will also learn how to order a large tree trunk or obtain large tree trunks for your pieces of work. The difference when working with natural wood and how it is different from milled wood.
F. **Step by step instruction** in carving your own chainsaw piece. You will see how the pros do it by seeing photos of unfinished pieces which show each step of the way.
G. **Using finishes on natural wood,** when working with natural tree wood, you will learn that depending on how fresh a tree has been cut, the wood might still be moist. You will learn how to properly dry your work before putting on a long lasting finish.

Chainsaw Safety

Before you get started with this marvelous art form, you need to know some basic safety tips when working with a chainsaw. Chainsaws come in all kinds of different sizes and their bars come in all kinds of different lengths. As you get proficient with your chainsaw carving, you might want to get several different sizes and bar lengths. The longer your bar and chain, the larger logs you are able to carve. You may need smaller chainsaws to carve smaller areas of the log.

Basic chainsaw safety basically follows common sense. You need to remember that a chainsaw can take off a limb or even cause fatal injuries if you are not careful using it. Some of the basic tips you need to know when carving with your chainsaw are listed below.

A. **Use safety goggles** when cutting with your chainsaw. Chainsaws typically throw rather large chips of wood, which can fly into your eyes and could harm them if they are not protected.
B. **Use hearing protection** if you have sensitive hearing.

C. **Maintain proper footing** when making a cut into the log with your chainsaw. A chainsaw does move with force, so you want to make sure that you have a stable enough footing to keep your balance while cutting with your chainsaw.
D. **Keep a safe distance from other people** when working with your chainsaw. We recommend that when you work with your chainsaw or have a series of chainsaws, you want to have a large enough space and not have people who are not working with you nearby and where they could get hit by flying debris from the chainsaw. You also want to keep small children away from the work area. If children want to watch you work on your chainsaw piece, you might want to designate a safe area for them where they won't be in harm's way.
E. **Avoid cutting with the nose of the bar,** as the nose of the bar can cause the chainsaw to kick back and the motor block could hit you in the face and cause skull fractures, eye loss, and other injuries.
F. **Hold the chainsaw with both hands** when carving. Working with a chainsaw requires a good amount of strength when running. The chain can cause strong kick back force as it cuts through the wood, especially when cutting through a knot.

Basic power tool safety is also important, because when doing chainsaw carving, your chainsaw is not the only tool you will need when cutting your log. Other power tools you will need include grills, a Dremel tool, sanders, power plains, and small rotary saws. Basic safety tips with smaller power tools are listed below.

A. **Safety goggles** are imperative with any power tool, not just chainsaws. Almost all power tools can throw debris into the direction of your eyes. Furthermore, when drilling, the bit can sometimes break and fly out. Sanders can throw fine saw dust into your eyes.
B. **Respirator or mouth and nose mask** should be worn when sanding if you have asthma or are sensitive to fine saw dust flying through the air.
C. **Follow instructions** for proper use of each tool.

Other Tools Needed for Chainsaw Carving
Because a chainsaw is designed as a broad cutting tool and not a tool to create fine works of art, you should only use a chainsaw for the larger cutting on the log. For example, when carving a bench out of a log, you use the chainsaw to cut out the sections for the flat part of the bench and the angular cuts to form the basic shapes of the other details on the side of the bench.

Keep in mind that a chainsaw is a cumbersome tool, and when carving out an indentation, such as your bench, you need to make a series of cuts which go straight down into the wood. Then you will have to get an angle cut into the one side and cut the wood out.

Drills are a necessity and are often used with large boring bits to allow for carving out the pupils of eyes and holes for nostrils.

The Dremel tool with router bits and rotary saw blades. The Dremel tool is a versatile tool which can be used in many small nooks and crannies which you will find on fingers, toes, paws, creases, etc.

Compact rotary wood saws can be used to saw small areas off to allow for realistic fingers, feet, claws, and other extremities you would find in a sculpture.

Wood augers are basically oversized drills. These are necessary when you are carving a bench, table, or other pieces which lay oblong and need legs. The wood auger has a large spiral bit which can drill holes between an inch to two inches in diameter.

Power and hand plains are needed to smooth cut notches and flat areas cut into the log, such as the seats of benches and chairs and the tops of tables.

Sometimes standard woodcarving knives are also necessary and to do fine tune work. You never know, but you may need a U-gouger or V-gouger to carve small enough grooves which a power tool cannot do. Keep in mind, however, most tree trunks which are used for chainsaw carving are hardwoods, primarily oak, but sometimes, they can be softwoods, like pine.

Sanders are imperative for smoothing out surfaces, especially if you are planning to use varnish or paints, as most chainsaw carvers do. There are different kinds of sanders you will need. Drum sanders will not work here, as drum sanders operate on a table which would not conform to the round and organic shapes of the natural logs. Other sanders used in chainsaw carving are listed below.

A. **The palm sander** is ideal for the type of surface which you will be working on with a chainsaw carving. The palm sander is a small flat sander which has an osculating flat sander base which is typically a square shape. The sandpaper is attached to the sander base with a couple lockable clips. You can change from corse to fine grit by switching the sandpaper. You need to keep in mind, however, natural wood is moist, so it can wear out your sandpaper much faster than dry wood.
B. **Corse and fine grit sanding bits** for the Dremel tool. In this project, your Dremel tool becomes a stylist and can get in to smooth off and even carve into the shapes of the eyes, nose, mouth, claws, fingers, toes, and more.

The History of Chainsaw or Log Carving

The history of chainsaw carving goes far, even to a time before there were chainsaws. What the chainsaw does to carve a log today was done with different axes and hatchets. In fact, many Native American tribes would carve logs into their religious symbols, this is especially true with the Pacific Northwest Indians.

The totem pole is the most famous log art created by the Pacific Northwest Indians. Basically, the Indian tribes of the Pacific northwest are different from the rest of the Native American population. Unlike all the Indian tribes in the US and Canada, who came across from the Russian far east over the frozen Barren Straights into Alaska and wondered further into the Americas, the Pacific Northwest Indians are believed to be of Polynesian origin from the Pacific southwest.

Like the Pacific Indians, the Polynesians also have experience in log carving. They still to this very day will carve their canoes out of the logs of tropical trees of the Pacific Islands and had totem poles which look very similar to those of the Pacific northwest.

Western expansion of both Canada and the United States introduced the art of log carving to people who settled in the West. For many people who built the first homesteads in the Wild west, log carving was a necessity as many homes were log cabins at the time. Over time, Native American log art began to influence many of the people of the Western territories.

When the Industrial Revolution took over America and the railroads were being built and as motors began to be much smaller than the typical massive steam engines which powered trains, generators, and many other vital industries which developed in the late 19th and early 20th Centuries, the chainsaw was invented.

Throughout the 20th Century, when people living out in the wilderness began to tame it and needed something to attract the crowd, the chainsaw not only played a pivotal role in the logging industry, but also in carving massive works of art from logs.

The chainsaw carving contests were introduced in the 1950s and 1960s and continue to this very day across the United States, especially out west. Some of these chainsaw carving contests are even broadcast on television and chainsaw carving has even become a million dollar business with chainsaw artists commissioning anywhere from 200 to 1,000 dollars per piece carved. Some chainsaw carvings can even cost over two thousand dollars if they have a lot of fine detail on them.

Becoming part of Americana is what made the art of chainsaw carving so popular today. Almost every home has a chainsaw carving of some kind their front yard, whether it is a name and address display, a yard sculpture of bears, indians, cowboys, and totem poles being the most popular genres.

Examples of Chainsaw Carvings

Chainsaw carvings have become so popular, as mentioned above, and the different genres of chainsaw carving are limitless. Seeing the different genres simply depicted in the chainsaw carvings shown in the images below will show you what you can learn what to do with natural logs.

Figure One: The Indian finished with an oil preservative

One of the traditional chainsaw carvings in a yard on Ponchartrain Trail in Michiana Shores, Indiana, this is a very common and popular genre of chainsaw carving. There are many chainsaw artists who carve logs into Indians or a common Native American motif. In some cases, part of the log can be used a pedestal as seen in this Indian carving.

Though the Native American motif is very popular, but it is not the only motif which is carved in chainsaw carving. In the same town in northern Indiana, at another house on Angle Road, the family is of Irish origin. The owners of the home with the chainsaw carving depicted in Figure Two below decided to have an Irish genre for their chainsaw carving by carving a leprechaun for their front yard.

Figure Two: A small chainsaw carving of an Irish leprechaun

As you can see in Figure Two above, this is a rather small chainsaw carving. This is a rather small log and would not take a large chainsaw to carve it. In a work like this one shown above, the chainsaw would only be used to carve the basic shape of this log.

In Figure Three below, you can see that you can get very creative when carving logs. At this home on Michiana Drive in Michiana, Michigan, a log was carved as a low bench with the look of an alligator.

Figure Three: Alligator shaped bench

As you can see in Figure Three above, this log was originally a curved log which was carved horizontally and had thinner logs placed as legs. This log carving seems like it had been painted white at one time to match the house, not shown in the photo.

As you can see, there is a lot you can do when you carve a log with a chainsaw. Once you get proficient with the techniques you learn in this chapter, you can let your imagination run wild and have some neat yard decorations which can be the envy of your neighbors.

Working with Natural Wood
While working with a chainsaw, you will be experiencing a completely different method of woodcarving than what you have learned thus far. The first thing you will need to understand is that when you are planning to carve logs using your chainsaw, you will be dealing with natural wood.

The one thing you need to understand when carving logs is that the wood might still be fresh. Some logs may still have fresh sap in them and others might still have moisture as they have been cut not too long ago. Wood is very porous and can hold water for a very long time. This is how trees are able to survive long dry spells. Furthermore, most logs will still have their bark on them when you get them, unless you have logs which are intended for building log cabins. Those logs usually have their bark shaved off before they get shipped to the builder.

Moisture can pose a problem for finishing and painting because varnishes, stains, and paints are specifically designed to bond to dry wood. It is Ok to carve the log with a chainsaw when it is still fresh and moist, as chainsaws are designed to cut live and dead wood, but you will want to dry the work before you begin to add your finishes or paints on the piece.

Drying your chainsaw carving is a special science in itself. Some logs can take as long as a whole month to dry, in humid areas, even longer. Do your carving first, then dry the work. The reason why we say that is because when you are carving your work, the bark will be coming off from the log. Furthermore, you may have to use a plain in some areas to get the bark off the log.

Bark is what primarily keeps the moisture in the wood. Consider the bark on a tree like its skin. Just like our skin gets rough and corse over time, especially when we do heavy manual labor most of our lives, the tree's bark works much the same way. As the bark stays on the log, it will hold moisture a lot longer than when the bark is removed.

If you are planning to put a finish on your carved log, we recommend that you do your chainsaw carving in a pole barn or other well ventilated enclosed area where you can use kerosene heaters to dry out the area and dry out the log.

When heat drying your chainsaw carving, you should use caution and not have the kerosene jet heaters too close to the work. Wood is temperamental and if you have the heaters too close to the work, it could crack. You want to slowly heat the work to allow it to dry slowly. Typically, if you dry your work with two kerosene jet heaters in the room, it should take a couple of weeks in normal weather conditions for your work to be completely dry. In humid conditions, you will want to wait for a month to be safe.

Step by Step Carving your Chainsaw Carving
When beginning your work, you will want to position your log in the way you want your work you want to stand when finished. This means that if you want your piece in an oblong position, such

as if you were carving a bench, as shown in Figure Three above, then you need to lay your log horizontally. If you want to carve a figure, like the Indian in Figure One or the Leprechaun in Figure Two, then you will want to position the log in a vertical position.

Note that if you want to have a free standing sculpture with your chainsaw carving, you might want to choose your logs properly. With free standing sculptures which are to be very tall and free standing, like in Figure One, you will want to get a rather large and wide log. If your carving something small, like the leprechaun in Figure Two, then you will want to get a smaller log which can stand stable.

Figure Four: Basic cutting of a log into a sculpture: photo from google images "Nowrthwoods Lifestyle Chainsaw Carving Archives"

Notice that in this image, this is the very beginning of the carving. You cannot be able to tell that this is going to be some kind of bird yet, but you can get a hunch as it begins to take its shape.
As you continue with your carving, simply use your chainsaw to carve away at the excess wood until you can get the basic shape of what you are carving.

In Figure Five, you can see that already, this work is not quite finished yet, but it is getting there. You can already tell that this is a bear and you can see that using the combination of the chainsaw and a rotary saw, you can notice the shape of the face, ears, and body, yet the eyes and other more detailed features need more work and smaller detail carving.

Figure Five: The progress of the wolf carving: Photo taken from Google Images from Garden Show Chainsaw Carving photo archives.

Notice here how the gentleman has already been carving away at the log and you can see the wolf begin to take its shape. Though you can begin to tell the details of the wolf, this work is far from being complete.

As you can see in Figure Five above, you can see that the wolf has almost taken its proper shape. You can even see a hint of the eyes. Notice that this gentleman also uses a special bar for his chainsaw. Many professional chainsaw carvers will use a special carving bar, as he is, but it is not really necessary.

In the same image in Figure Five above, you can also notice a second man who is carving a woman or possibly a mermaid. Like the man carving the wolf in the front of the image, the work of the man in the back is still far from completion and still requires more work.

There is one caveat when you are using the nose of your chainsaw bar to carve with, however. Chainsaws do have a lot of power when they are running and you also need to understand that the RPM speed of the gear which drives the chain around the bar is so fast that if it were attached to a vehicle, such as a go cart, it would be going 45 miles an hour. Knowing this, the chainsaw bar nose is also where the blades on the chain begin to go to the top and the cutting edge does not completely dig into the wood as they do on the bottom of the bar. This can cause some strong kick back if you are not careful. Chainsaws are dangerous tools to work with and if the kick back is strong enough, it can knock your chainsaw out of your hands, or it can fly back and hit you in the eye, break your nose, or do other serious damage. Keep this in mind when anticipating using the nose of your chainsaw bar.

According to the article from SFGate, featuring the above photo from SFGate, Mark Tyoe is a professional, so he does know how to handle the kick back of the chainsaw. Furthermore, the carving blade also has a different shape as a regular bar. It has more of a point to it, thus this can reduce the kickback from the chainsaw.

Using the rotary saw can create almost the same effects as tip carving with the chainsaw and is much safer, especially for beginners. What is nice about using the rotary saw to do what Mark Tyoe is doing is that a rotary saw is more compact, is designed to do more delicate work, and has much less kickback than the powerful motor of a chainsaw.

In many cases, you might not be able to get that special carving bar for your chainsaw, thus using the more common rounded nose of a typical chainsaw bar you find at any hardware or home improvement store has a broader curve, and is incapable of doing such detail work. Sometimes, you might even be able to use some of the carving bits which come with your Dremel tool to do some of the same details.

Figure Six: Image taken from Google Images, Dusseldorf Kettensager Georg Maurus

If you notice in Figure Six, this man is using a rotary saw to do some of the fine detail work. For even finer detail, you can also use the Dremel tool for finer carving of eyes, nostrils, and more.

You can use the Dremel tool to do the finest detail of your chainsaw sculpture. When using your Dremel tool, you can use a mixture of both router bits, engraving bits, and some of the pointed sanding bits to fine tune the surface of your chainsaw carving.

Using Finishes on Natural Wood
After carving your sculpture and you are satisfied about how it looks, then it's time to choose a finish for it. As mentioned above, logs are natural wood and have not been milled. Basically, when you are undertaking chainsaw carving, you have to realize that logs come in different sizes, with bark, or stripped from their bark. It all depends where you buy your logs from. You can also go out into the woods if you have enough land and chop down a tree and use the trunk of that tree for your carving as well. Some logs may even have moss on their bark. Use care with these logs. Typically, moss is a sign of moisture and you want to attempt to avoid as much moisture as possible.

Moisture is your worst enemy when you are looking to finish your work. You need to understand that wood is porous and can suck up moisture like a sponge. There are several problems that moisture can cause with most finishes and these are listed below.

A. **Moisture can cause rot** in the wood. Rot is not a good thing. Rot will eventually break down the molecular structure of your wooden sculpture and this makes the wood become soft. If you have ever been in the woods and picked up some sticks and they break upon impact when you drop them on the ground, this is a sign that the wood from this stick is rotten. What happens when wood rots is that different bacteria, fungi, and other micro organisms will break down the cellulose structure of the wood and grains will disappear and the wood will begin to flake apart. Also, if you ever break a piece of wood which is rotten or semi rotten, you will notice that the rings or the grains are not as defined as in good solid wood. In the case of finished wood, you can have dry rot if the wood is not completely dried before you apply the finish. What exactly is dry rot? Well, dry rot is called that because it is when you think your work is completely dry because it is dry to the touch, but it actually is not. It can still be moist deep in the heart wood. This then rots from inside out and it takes several years before you notice it.
B. **Insects** can be another problem when your wood is moist. Insects love moisture and when you have moisture in your chainsaw carving, this can attract wood roaches, termites, carpenter ants, and other insects. Insects can cause a problem which is similar to rot. What insects can do is burrow into the wood itself and chew out the cellulose structure which the wood is made from at the molecular level. In a way, insects can also cause rot, as they use enzymes in their saliva when they chew the wood which break it down. Likewise, when insects burrow into the wood, they sometimes breed inside and their larvae can also cause the wood to rot. If the wood is very dry, insects will not be attracted to it.
C. **Pealing** can be a big problem if you choose to paint your chainsaw carvings. The fact is that painting can be very temperamental. As mentioned before, when working with paints on wood, you will need primers and if the wood is still moist, the primer might not bond well to the surface.
D. **Stains and varnishes** work well because they get sucked up into the pores of the wood. If there is moisture in the wood, then the pores are already filled, thus you might have a problem with the stains and varnishes. The stains might begin to beed up because they

cannot get into the porous surface of the wood. Varnish is sticky when wet, so it might apply on, but because enough of it cannot get in the pores, it will begin to peal shortly after dried.

As mentioned above, you want to keep your unfinished pieces in a dry ventilated area. To properly do chainsaw carving, you should have a large area, such as a pole barn or area which is well ventilated and protected from the elements when drying out your piece. Though your carving can already begin to dry as you are carving it, since the bark coming off will allow the moisture to evaporate more quickly. Humid climates, however, can also make it take longer for the moisture to come out. The best thing you can to is to have kerosene heaters slowly dry the work out. The thicker and bigger the log is, the longer it will take to dry out.

Wood burning is a great way to add character to your chainsaw carving. There are many ways you can burn in color and create a darker look by charing your work. There are a series of different tools which you can use when burning specific areas in your chainsaw carving and some of the most popular tools are listed below.

A. **A soldering iron** is your fine detail burning tool. Basically, a soldering iron is a metal rod which gets very hot to melt led wiring to solder pieces of metal together and is often used in delicate metal work, stained and leaded glass work. Because a soldering iron gets hot enough to melt lead and other soft metals used in soldering, it can be used to burn wood. You want to use care in using a soldering iron as it can cause a fire if you leave it around paper and flammable liquids, such as stains and varnishes.
B. **A blow torch** is a great tool for burning and charing large areas of your carving. When using a blow torch for burning in color into your work, you want to make sure that you have a special blow torch which has a control valve on the flame throwing nozzle. Most blow torches run on propane gas and have a special tank which allows the fuel for the fire. Some blow torches are simply fixed to the top of the tank and can be cumbersome to use. There are other blow torches designed for detail work in a wide variety of different trades which have a flexible hose from the fuel tank to the nozzle. This is the kind of blow torch you want for wood burning. These kinds of blow torches also have adjustable flow valves on the nozzles which you can adjust the flame to the area you want to burn. Typically, nozzles get turned on by lighting a match and turning the gas on and holding the flame of the match to the nozzle. The gas ignites and you have your flame.

If you are looking for a natural finish with some light and dark areas, then wood burning and staining can be a great combination for your chainsaw carving. What can be nice about wood burning is that you can make areas somewhat dark or very dark, depending on the extent of the heat you apply to the wood. Do not use wood burning tools around your stains or varnishes. Do the wood burning first, as the stains and varnishes are highly flammable. Furthermore, not only are the stains and varnishes flammable themselves, but their fumes can also catch fire if you are not careful. Burn first, then apply the stains and varnishes.

Chainsaw carving can be a great hobby and is the epitome of the ultimate hard core woodcarving. This is an art form which has evolved over the centuries when it was simply log carving with the use of axes, hatchets, and tomahawks to massive chainsaws. The carvings have also evolved from ancient religious symbols and deities to newer more kitsch, such as mermaids, bears, indians, fish, alligators, and more. Chainsaw carving does test your muscles and can also be amazing when you get proficient at it.

Epilogue

Well, if you have come this far, then you seem to be serious about woodcarving. You already know all the different techniques of woodcarving that are available. You have learned everything from chip and relief carving as the basis for all two dimensional carving to three dimensional carving, which includes figurines, chainsaw carving, and making bowls, spoons, and other vessels out of wood.

In the Epilogue, you will learn all the different techniques for carving, the basics of composition, and other methods to turn your work in to a work of art which can make everyone admire it. Some of the extra tips and techniques you will learn in the Epilogue include the following:

A. **Wood burning,** which was covered in Chapter Nine about chainsaw carving. You can also do finer wood burning on your smaller works, such as chip and relief carvings, some figurines, bowls, and other wood pieces. You will learn how to burn designs in your woodcarving or enhance some carved areas by using a simple soldering iron which you can find at any hobby shop.
B. **Treating wood with olive or vegetable oil** for wood pieces used in cooking and food preparation. This especially applies to wood cutting boards, bowls, and spoons used in cooking. You will learn about the porousness of wood and why it is important that wood can only be used with certain foods. You will learn why carved functional pieces, such as cutting boards and vessels should never be used in the dish washer or washed in water. You will also know about the fault pas of cutting meats and chicken on a wood cutting board.
C. **Proper care of woodcarving pieces** depending on a wide variety of environmental conditions. Wood can be very susceptible to humidity and moisture. Have you ever had that wooden door which was so difficult to open or that window which won't open anymore? Well, you will learn about the porous nature of wood and how humidity and moisture can cause wood to expand and contract. You will know why wood sometimes cracks, warps, and can split due to the changes in humidity and moisture levels are. This especially affects musical instruments and you will know why many wooden string instruments, such as guitars, lutes, and other string instruments you learned in this book should be tuned every once in a while. Warping of the wood and tight strings can also have tension on the wood which can also cause the top of your sound box to sometimes crack.
D. **Proper climate control** needed for wooden musical instruments which you have hand carved. This is crucial for those of you who are musically inclined and want to learn woodcarving to make musical instruments. You will learn about special storage rooms you can create with special dehumidifiers and thermostats to control both heat and humidity in the area where you store your instruments. This is crucial to keep warping and cracking.
E. **Joining woodcarving clubs and guilds** is a great way to meet all kinds of different woodcarvers in your area. If this is a hobby you want to seriously pursue, woodcarving clubs and guilds can allow you to know other woodcarvers who have more experience, get ideas for projects, and more.
F. **Tips on sharpening your knives** so you always have a sharp knife to carve with. Sharpening is a very tricky thing to do. You need to understand that having the proper angle when sharpening knives is imperative to have a knife razor sharp. Sometimes, this

might not be something you want to take on yourself, thus you should have several knives and gougers of the same size so you have a spare to work with when the other set is dull. You will learn about the different sharpeners which are available and what you need to look at if you choose to hire a professional sharpener to sharpen your knives. You will also learn about honing and why it is so important. You will learn about the proper honing surfaces and how it fine tunes your edge.

Wood Burning

Many woodcarvers will use a technique known as *wood burning* to enhance carved pieces and give them more character. What exactly is wood burning? Well, basically, wood burning is charing certain areas of your woodcarving to burn in a pattern or to enhance a carved pattern by charing a specific area and making it darker than the rest of the wood.

Wood burning is actually an art form of its own and many serious woodworkers will call it *pyrography*, which basically defines engraving an image into the wood using a source of heat. Typically, wood burning is done with a hot iron, such as a soldering iron, but if you want to do some intricate wood burning to enhance your carving, we recommend you get a wood burning tool kit. These tools work much like a soldering iron. It is an electrical tool which has a built in heating coil that heats a metal tip that can be changed. Many wood burning tools can come with a wide variety of sizes from large to small.

Pyrography safety is important. Any pyrography or wood burning tool does get hot. You want to make sure you use a pyrography pen or wood burning tool which can get over 451° Fahrenheit. This is the kindling temperature for paper, wood shavings, and flammable liquids, such as different finishes, such as stains and varnishes, paints, and primers. Put your wood burning tool on the wrong place on your workbench, you can have a major fire on your hands. Some of the safety tips don't just apply to pyrography, but are simple common sense, however, when using wood burning tools, you should follow the tips below.

A. **Keep varnishes, stains, paints, primers, and glues in a metal container.** Many of the woodworking chemicals, as the ones mentioned above are highly flammable and some of them even have flammable fumes. With this in mind, you should safely store all your finishes, glues, and cleansers in a special metal container. You can find special storage closets at any Home Depot, Menard's, Lowe's, or any other home improvement or hobby shop made specifically for the storage of flammable liquids. These metal closets are basically like a free standing armoire with two doors which open towards the middle. Most of these metal storage units have special valves which can release if flammable fumes can release if they build up. You can also find these storage units at any automotive store who markets to people who like to work on cars. These are made for gasoline as well. Not only should you store your flammable liquids in such a storage unit, but also brushes and rags used for varnishing and staining.
B. **Never keep your wood burning tools plugged in unattended.** Pyrography deals with hot tools. If you leave your wood burning tools plugged in, even just to go to the bathroom, can cause a fire if the conditions are right.
C. **Never do pyrography** in the same area where you use saws, carve, or have papers around. It is a good idea to have a separate pyrography station where you do all your wood burning.

Stencils are an ideal tool for wood burning. In fact, back in the day, when merchandise was delivered in wood crates, messages on the crates, such as *This side up* or *Fragile* were often stenciled and burned onto the wood. This can be great for those of you who want to have an old fashion look for rooms or other projects.

Using a fine tipped pyrography pen is ideal for intricate wood burning on vessels and other items where wood burning can give you the right look for your projects. This can be ideal for carved bowls, storage vessels, and other items you choose to have as either house decorations or as functional pieces. If you look at Figure One below, you can see a perfect example of pyrography on this Russian wood vessel carved out of basswood.

Figure One: Russian basswood vessels we acquired on one of our many trips to Russia
    Figure 1a   Figure 1b   Figure 1c

Notice in all three of these images in Figure One what you can do with wood burning. If you get a high quality pyrography pen, you also have some knife blades which allow you to carve into the wood as you are burning it at the same time. This can give you engraved lines and chips as seen with the lines in the vessels portrayed above. As you can see, the vessels in Figures 1a and 1b, the vessels have never been varnished or stained. Figure 1c does illustrate how a basswood vessel would look like with a coat of varnish without stain. Also notice the beautiful chip carving detail and how nicely it works together with the wood burned design on the vessel.

Treating Wood with Olive or Vegetable Oil
If you want to learn woodcarving to make things for food preparation, such as cutting boards, bowls, utensils, and other items, then you do not want to use any toxic stains and varnishes to finish your works.

Dangers of using wood for food preparations can be quite serious. The reason why wood cutting boards and vessels should be heavily oiled is because of the porous nature of wood. Scientific studies have concluded that in a wooden handle of a kitchen knife alone, there is more bacteria than in a public bathroom. This gives to reason that a cutting board can be a good breading ground for bacteria as well.

Meats should never be worked with on a wooden cutting board because of the juices from the meats can be quickly absorbed by the wood. Furthermore, especially dangerous is preparing chicken on a wood cutting board because chicken juices can cause the outbreak of salmonella, which can be a deadly disease.

Ideal uses for wood cutting boards include the preparation of dough, preparing and chopping vegetables, or fruits. These tend to be more dry, so liquids won't be absorbed. Furthermore, if the boards are oiled, the juices from fruits and vegetables won't be as absorbed. Wood bowls vessels can be great for mixing and storing spices, salt, pepper, etc.

Proper Care of Woodcarving Pieces
The environment can be quite harsh on wood. Basically, to understand the proper care of your work or woodwork in general, you need to understand the properties of wood. Basics you need to know about wood and why proper care and storage are listed below.

A. **The porousness of wood** is the biggest factor of wood and why wood behaves the way it does. Because wood is porous, wood is able to imbibe moisture, liquids, and will take so long to dry. This is why wood boats need a strong spar urethane varnish before it can be put in the water.
B. **Wood expands and contracts** because of the porous structure of the wood. The reason why wood expands and contracts the way it does is because as the temperature rises and dives during the change of the seasons, the molecular structure of the wood is designed to do the same. Basically, when wood becomes saturated with moisture during a hot and humid summer, it can expand and thus will cause the situation, such as a sticking door, windows which can't open, etc. Likewise, when it gets cooler and dryer, wood can contract, making it easier to open the door or window. The problem is that wood not only expands and contracts, but it can also warp. When warping happens, this can cause musical instruments to pop, snap, or crack open. Warping can also cause wood panels which are made from different pieces of wood glued together to come apart.

Musical instruments need the most special care. If you want to learn woodcarving because you want to make musical instruments, such as lutes, guitars, or other wooden string instruments, you need to understand that the fluctuation of temperature and ambient humidity can adversely affect the instruments you make.

Climate controlled rooms and storage areas are a necessity for the proper care of musical instruments. If you ever get the chance to visit a professional music school or a performing arts center and get to visit the area where they store their prize instruments, such as Stratevarian violins, you will notice that these rooms have special dehumidifiers and meters which control humidity and temperature. This is very important. Have you ever wondered how woodworkers are able to bend wood without breaking it? Well, it is done by placing them in a steamed area to saturate the wood with moisture. This makes the wood pliable and using special jigs, a woodworker is able to bend it to the desirable shape.

Think of your instruments as being a work of wood with its own jig. Most string instruments have strings which are tightly pulled to make the desired note. This puts a lot of stress on the wood and when the conditions are right, the wood can be bent to a point and then warps and snaps. This needs to be curbed by special climate control which you will read about below.

Tuning is often done with any wooden string instrument or wooden instruments which are percussion instruments with strings, such as pianos. What happens as wood expands and contracts, it will stretch some of the strings and over time, the strings will loose their tightness and the sound of the note the string will make changes.

When tuning your home made instruments, you can get tuners at any music store which can be set to detect a certain note. Use one of these devices to tune your instrument.

Proper Climate Control for Woodcarving Pieces
Basically, most woodcarvings simply need a lukewarm dry environment to remain well preserved. If your works are varnished with a good urethane, then you should not have too much to worry about. The problem lies with musical instruments and any kind of woodwork which can be adversely affected with the slightest environmental changed.

Climate control can be easily done by using a dehumidifier and having special instruments which can measure temperature, humidity, and set your climate control machines until the humidity levels are at the desired level. Note, however, that special climate control devices can be very costly in both purchase and usage of electricity.

Joining Woodcarving Clubs and Guilds
For many, woodcarving can be a difficult hobby to begin. There are many different woodcarving clubs and guilds around which allow people who enjoy woodcarving to share ideas, advice, and tips can be a great way for you to improve your skill. Many of the bigger woodcarving clubs and guilds also offer woodcarving classes, workshops, and other events where you have the opportunity to improve your woodcarving skills.

Proper Knife Sharpening
To do quality woodcarving, you need a sharp set of knives. Woodcarving knives are different from your average kitchen or pocket knives. Woodcarving knives and gougers have special blades with special shapes, thus they have to be razor sharp to be able to cut into the wood without chipping it and removing more than they are supposed to.

Seeking a professional sharpener is recommended for those of you who do not understand cutlery and how to properly sharpen a blade. This is crucial, because you can irreparably ruin your expensive woodcarving knives and gougers if you sharpen them improperly. You need to understand the proper angles, thus a professional tool sharpener who knows the proper angles and has the proper tools should be hired. This is why you should have two spare sets of carving knives and gougers when you are doing a woodcarving piece. The more detailed and the larger your piece is, the more likely you will have to go to your spare set while doing the work.

Woodcarving is a wonderful hobby and can be very relaxing. There is nothing more fulfilling than having an outlet for your creativity and to know an art form which is both beautiful and functional.

Made in the USA
Lexington, KY
17 May 2019